LONDON WALKS

SEE THE CITY LIKE A LOCAL

CONTENTS

WALKS

outhend ✈→

City ✈→

1000 m

THE BEST OF LONDON IN 6 WALKS

WALK **1** > WESTMINSTER, ST. JAMES'S & MAYFAIR p.18

This is the London you see on postcards—Buckingham Palace, Westminster Abbey, and the London Eye.

WALK **2** > SOUTHWARK p.38

Southwark has its fair share of popular London attractions, including Tower Bridge, Tate Modern, and Borough Market.

WALK **3** > SHOREDITCH p.58

This neighborhood showcases London's creative side. Mingle with London's hip crowd in one-of-a-kind shops and markets.

WALK **4** > KING'S CROSS & ANGEL p.78

Recent years have been good to King's Cross—great new spots are popping up right and left. Angel is a young, dynamic area that will take you off the beaten path.

WALK **5** > MARYLEBONE, REGENT'S PARK & PRIMROSE HILL p.98

Marylebone High Street is a favorite shopping destination among Londoners, and Primrose Hill is a hidden corner of the city with a laid-back vibe and a small-town feel.

WALK **6** > KNIGHTSBRIDGE & CHELSEA p.118

Some of London's most expensive homes are in Knightsbridge and Chelsea, and this is reflected in the shops and restaurants.

LONDON WALKS

Step off the plane and head right for the newest, hippest café in town. Discover where to get the best fish and chips in the city or where to find locally brewed beer on tap. In *Moon London Walks,* local authors share with you genuine high-lights of the city they love. This way, you can skip the busy shopping streets and stroll through the city at your own pace, taking in a local attraction on your way to the latest and greatest shops. Savor every second and make your city trip a true feel-good experience.

LONDON-BOUND!

You're about to discover London, one of our favorite cities. The charming neigh-borhoods, amazing museums, and fabulous galleries are inspiring, and we love all of the shopping possibilities—from big, beautiful department stores to small, independent boutiques. Booking a table at the restaurant of a celebrity chef or cookbook author is pretty cool, too, not to mention the city's many great mar-kets, view from the London Eye, old-school boat rides over the Thames, and all the trendy cocktail bars mixing up perfect gin and tonics. Winter, spring, summer, and fall—London buzzes year-round.

ABOUT THIS BOOK

In this book, local authors share with you the genuine highlights of the city they love. Discover the city by foot and at your own pace, so you can relax and expe-rience the local lifestyle without having to do a lot of preparation beforehand. That means more time for you—what we call "time to momo." Our walks take you past our favorite restaurants, cafés, museums, galleries, shops, and other notable attractions—places we ourselves like to go.

None of the places mentioned here have paid to appear in either the text or the photos, and all text has been written by an independent editorial staff. This is true for the places in this book as well as for the information in the **time to momo app** and all the latest tips, themed walks, neighborhood information, blogs, and the selection of best hotels on **www.timetomomo.com.**

CITY
LONDON

WORK & ACTIVITIES
MARKETING MANAGER

Kim studied fashion in Amsterdam and London. She loves vintage boutiques, pop-up markets, and decadent depart-

LOCAL
KIM SNIJDERS

ment stores. Her favorite things to do in London include practicing yoga, playing ping-pong, going bowling, catching a movie at the secret cinema, and wandering through the city. She also regularly visits the exhibitions at the Tate Modern and V&A.

PRACTICAL INFORMATION

The six walks in this book allow you to discover the best neighborhoods in the city by foot and at your own pace. The walks will take you past museums and notable attractions but, more importantly, they'll show you where to go for great food and drinks, shopping, entertainment, and an overall good time. Check out the map at the front of this book to see which areas of the city the walks will take you through.

Each route is clearly indicated on a detailed map at the beginning of the relevant chapter. The map also specifies where each listing is located. The color of the number tells you what type of venue it is (see the key at the bottom of this page). A description of each place is given later in the chapter.

Without taking into consideration extended stops at various locations, each walk will take a maximum of three hours. The approximate distance is indicated at the top of the page, before the directions.

PRICE INDICATION
We give an idea of how much you can expect to spend at each location along with its address and contact details. Unless otherwise stated, the amount given in restaurant listings is the average price of a main course. For sights and attractions, we indicate the cost of a regular full-price ticket. Any reduced rates that may be available are not listed.

```
                            LEGEND

    ● >> SIGHTS & ATTRACTIONS      ● >> FOOD & DRINK
    ● >> SHOPPING                  ● >> MORE TO EXPLORE
```

GOOD TO KNOW

Most stores in London are open seven days a week, usually from 10am until 8pm with shorter hours on Sunday. There are exceptions, of course, so always make sure to check the opening hours at your destination before you head out. On public holidays, or "bank holidays" as they are called in England, most stores remain open and public transportation still runs, but expect shorter Sunday hours.

Restaurants often automatically add a 10 to 15 percent gratuity to your bill. Although leaving a tip isn't required, it is customary—but double-check your bill to be sure that you don't end up tipping twice. If no gratuity has been added to your check, it's expected that you'll leave about a 10 percent tip.

London has strict smoking laws. Smoking is banned in enclosed public spaces, including hotels, bars, restaurants, theaters, and on public transportation.

Whenever possible, book tickets for the train and any sights and attractions in advance. Online prices are often significantly lower than what you'll pay at the door.

TYPICAL LONDON

A typical English breakfast is the "full English" or "fry-up," and consists of fried eggs, bacon, toast, and baked beans.

In London, as in the rest of England, a relatively elaborate Sunday lunch is a well-established tradition. Known as a Sunday roast, this meal includes meat, potatoes, vegetables, and Yorkshire pudding.

Another great tradition is, of course, afternoon tea, which is not to be confused with high tea. Afternoon tea takes place around 4pm and consists of a combination of sweet and savory bites along with a cup of tea. High tea, on the other hand, is essentially a simple evening meal.

Londoners drink their fair share of tea—preferably strong black tea with a splash of milk. This popular drink is known here as "builder's tea."

PUBLIC HOLIDAYS

Public holidays are referred to as "bank holidays" in the UK because banks are closed on these days. Many of these bank holidays are on Mondays. In addition to days like Good Friday and Easter Monday, which don't fall on a specific date, the following are official holidays in the UK:

January 1 > New Year's Day
First Monday in May > Early May Bank Holiday
Last Monday in May > Spring Bank Holiday
Last Monday in August > Summer Bank Holiday
December 25 > Christmas Day
December 26 > Boxing Day

HAVE ANY TIPS?

We've put a lot of care into this guidebook. Yet shops and restaurants in London come and go fairly regularly. We do our best to keep the walks and contact details as up to date as possible, and this is reflected in our digital products. We update the print edition as often as possible. However, if, despite our best efforts, there is a place that you can't find or if you have any other comments or tips about this book, please email info@momedia.nl, or leave a message at **www.timetomomo.com.**

TUNED IN TO LONDON!

GO TO WWW.TIMETOMOMO.COM FOR THE LATEST TIPS
NEW ADDRESSES + UP-AND-COMING NEIGHBORHOODS
+ POP-UP STORES + CONCERTS + FESTIVALS + MUCH MORE

TRANSPORTATION

The train or bus will get you downtown within 45 minutes from any of London's five **airports.** Expect to pay about £15 each way for the train, and about £10 for the bus. A taxi will set you back at least £55. Train information is available at *www.thetrainline.com*. From Heathrow and London City Airports you can take the subway, referred to locally as "the Underground" or "the Tube," into the city for about £4.50.

If you're traveling by **Eurostar** via the Channel Tunnel, you'll arrive at St. Pancras International railway station. From here you can easily take the Tube or bus to any corner of the city.

Once in central London, the fastest way to get around is with the **Underground.** Buy an **Oyster card** for £10 and save on subway, bus, and certain train tickets. The average fare for a Tube ride, for example, costs £4.80 without an Oyster card but just £2.30 with one. You can purchase a prepaid Oyster card online and at most stations. The card is easy to use; just swipe it whenever you enter or leave a station. For more information, check out *www.tfl.gov.uk*. A map of the London Underground is available in the back of this book.

The **bus** is a great way to see the city. A ride to or from central London costs £1.50 with an Oyster card. The destination is clearly indicated on the front of every bus, together with some of the stops along the way. London also has an extensive network of night buses. See *www.tfl.gov.uk/buses* for more details.

Thanks to the open **double-decker tour buses,** it's even possible to see a good deal of London's most notable attractions in a couple of hours in one easy loop. Various companies run tours leaving from Victoria, Trafalgar Square, Piccadilly, and other popular tourist destinations, but the Original Tour is a good option. Tickets cost £27 online, and there are plenty of hop-on, hop-off stops to choose from. See *www.theoriginaltour.com*.

Taxis, or "black cabs" as they are called in London, are easy to hail by sticking out your hand. A taxi is available when the top light is on. Taxis offer an affordable way to travel when you're with three or more people and aren't traveling far. Minicabs, or private taxis, are cheaper but aren't always as reliable. You can't just hail a minicab on the street—they need to be booked in advance—and if one randomly stops and offers its services, you'd do best not to take it. Use whatever company your hotel uses instead. Prices should be agreed on beforehand.

You can also get around quickly in London by **boat.** There are many options for water travel, from speedy line services to slow leisure cruises. Find out more at *www.tfl.gov.uk/river* and *www.thamesclippers.com* for high-speed boats.

BIKING

Despite the heavy left-hand traffic and the lack of bike lanes, biking is becoming increasingly more popular in London. This is thanks in part to former mayor Boris Johnson, who used to cycle to work himself, launched the city's **bike-share** system, Santander Cycles, and oversaw the creation of multiple-cycle super-highways. Be sure to stay alert while riding because cars and buses don't always look out for bikers, either because they're not used to them or simply out of frustration, and Londoners often tend to ride fast and sometimes carelessly. Helmets are not required but are recommended. Also note that, unlike in other parts of Europe, it's uncommon to park your bike on the side of the road in London.

Renting a bike in London can be great fun. Walks 5 and 6 through Marylebone, Regent's Park & Primrose Hill, and Knightsbridge & Chelsea are particularly well suited for cycling. Rent a Santander Cycle, locally referred to as a "Boris bike." These bikes are available across the city and are easy to rent from a docking station using a credit card. Rates start at £2 per day. The first half hour is free, and each additional half hour costs £2. Visit *www.tfl.gov.uk/cycling* for more information and nice bike routes.

1 Start the day with breakfast at **Plum + Spilt Milk.** > p. 85

2 Check out interactive exhibits at the **Science Museum.** > p. 122

3 Take a walk, ride a bike, fly a kite, or have a picnic in **Regent's Park.** > p. 114

4 Rise above the city in the **London Eye** and admire the view. > p. 36

5 See the gorillas and other animals at the **London Zoo.** > p. 117

6 Visit the Queen at **Buckingham Palace.** > p. 22

7 Enjoy afternoon tea at **The Berkeley** hotel.> p. 129

8 Order fish and chips in **The Old Red Cow** pub. > p. 49

9 Bask in the botanical splendor at **Kew Gardens.** > p. 138

10 Shop at **Liberty,** one of London's best-loved department stores. > p. 34

TOP 10 | RESTAURANTS

1 Enjoy a Mediterranean meal at **Ottolenghi.** > p. 89

2 Order a traditional Sunday roast at **Roast.** > p. 49

3 Choose between surf and turf at **Burger & Lobster.** > p. 50

4 Head to **Bumpkin** for classic British fare. > p. 126

5 **Manna** is one of the best vegetarian restaurants in the city. > p. 109

6 Discover Peruvian cuisine at **Andina.** > p. 65

7 Veggies take center stage at **Grain Store.** > p. 85

8 **Momo** serves up delicious North African dishes in a lively atmosphere. > p. 30

9 Dine in style at the upscale **Mews of Mayfair.** > p. 30

10 Go to **KIN** for affordable Asian food. > p. 50

1 Marvel at burlesque and cabaret at **House of Burlesque.** > 27 Old Gloucester Street

2 Mingle with Dalston hipsters at **Cafe OTO.** > 18-22 Ashwin Street

3 Drink in a former train station at **Oslo.** > 1a Armhurst Road

4 **Union Chapel** is an amazing music venue. > Compton Terrace

5 Cocktails at former air raid shelter **Cahoots.** > 13 Kingly Court

6 **Queen of Hoxton** is a bar, club, and art gallery. > 1-5 Curtain Road

7 Head to **Bounce** for ping-pong, food, and drinks. > 121 Holborn

8 Something different every night at **93 Feet East.** > 150 Brick Lane

9 Drink in style at **Happiness Forgets.** > 8-9 Hoxton Square

10 **Proud Camden** is a club located in a former horse hospital. > Camden Market

TOP 10 | MARKETS

1 Enjoy the vibe and tasty snacks at **Borough Market.** > p. 54

2 Vintage pieces and great food at **Sunday Upmarket.** > p. 74

3 Shop for antiques at **Alfies Antique Market.** > p. 113

4 Bustling and colorful **Columbia Road Flower Market.** > p. 74

5 Check out the famous **Portobello Road Market.** > p. 138

6 Secondhand items and souvenirs at **Spitalfields Market.** > p. 73

7 Sample street food and other tasty snacks at **Maltby Street Market.** > p. 46

8 Mix with London's hippest at **Broadway Market.** > p. 74

9 **Chelsea Farmers Market** is a collection of great restaurants and charming shops. > p. 134

10 **Kerb Food** has the best food trucks in town. > p. 86

WALK **1**

WESTMINSTER, ST. JAMES'S & MAYFAIR

ABOUT THE WALK

This walk takes you past all the sights London is most famous for. Much of the focus is on history and culture, but there are also plenty of good shopping opportunities along the way. Upscale restaurants and hotels allow you to enjoy a nice dinner or afternoon tea. The walk is fairly long, so consider biking the middle section through St. James's Park if you want to save time.

THE NEIGHBORHOODS

Westminster lies on the north bank of the River Thames and is the iconic London featured on postcards. Numerous places in Westminster are included on UNESCO's World Heritage List, and the area is incredibly popular among tourists. Great Britain has been ruled from this corner of London from as early as the 11th century. It's home to political and religious power hubs such as the **Houses of Parliament, Downing Street,** and **Westminster Abbey.** The most famous part of the Houses of Parliament is the bell tower and clock referred to as **Big Ben.** The Palace of Westminster, home to Parliament, was originally built in the 11th century. Due to a fire in 1834, however, most of the current structure dates to around 1840. South of Westminster you'll find St. James's Park and **Buckingham Palace,** the top royal attraction in the city. Since Queen Victoria made it her home in 1837, Buckingham Palace has been the official residence of the British monarchy. Today the Queen is nearly the sole resident of this part of London—the stately buildings in this area are primarily home to upscale businesses, government offices, and ultra-expensive unoccupied apartments.

North of St. James's Park lie the posh neighborhoods St. James's and Mayfair. In addition to the beautiful historical buildings and elegant squares here, these neighborhoods are also known for their social clubs (traditional gentlemen's clubs) and perfectly tailored suits. Since 1800 **Savile Row** has been one of the best-known streets for tailor-made clothing and custom shoes. **Bond Street** and New Bond Street in Mayfair are also home to the shops of famous high-end fashion brands. The luxury boutiques, jewelry shops, and antique stores here are a shopping paradise for those with an accommodating wallet. You'll also find a number of famous art institutions and auction houses in St. James's and Mayfair, including the **Royal Academy,** Christie's, and Sotheby's.

SHORT ON TIME? HERE ARE THE HIGHLIGHTS
+ LONDON EYE + BUCKINGHAM PALACE + TRAFALGAR SQUARE
+ BOND STREET + AFTERNOON TEA AT CLARIDGE'S

TIPS
// Ideal for first-time visitors
// The many sights and attractions make this a great Sunday walk
// This long route is suitable for biking

SIGHTS & ATTRACTIONS

② The Palace of Westminster, better known as the **Houses of Parliament,** is a labyrinth of over 1,000 stately rooms from which the British government conducts its routine business. Visitors will easily recognize the giant clock tower known as Big Ben. The palace was originally built in the late 11th century, but due to a fire in 1834, most of the current structure dates to around 1840. Tours of the palace are possible during Parliament's summer recess, and reservations are required. You can also attend a debate.

parliament square, sw1, www.parliament.uk, t: 02072194114, see website for visiting hours, price tour £25, tube westminster

④ The **Jewel Tower** is one of the few remaining parts of the original medieval palace that now forms the Houses of Parliament. At the time, the tower was built to store the king's jewels and treasures. Today it houses an exhibition on the history of the British parliament.

parliament square, sw1, www.english-heritage.org.uk, t: 02072222219, see website for opening hours, entrance £4.20, tube westminster

⑤ The beautiful Gothic church **Westminster Abbey**—where Prince William and Kate Middleton were married—is something of a covered graveyard. Over the past 1,000 years, many famous kings and queens have been buried here, along with numerous poets, scientists, musicians, and soldiers. Services here are open to the public.

20 deans yard, sw1, www.westminster-abbey.org, t: 02072225152, open mon-tue & thu-fri 9:30am-3:30pm, wed 9:30am-6pm, sat 9:30am-2:30pm, entrance £20, tube westminster/st. james's park

⑧ **Buckingham Palace** has been the official residence of the British monarchy since Queen Victoria moved here in 1837. A selection of the palace's 775 rooms are open to the public in August and September. Most visitors, however, come here to see the Changing of the Guard.

st. james's park, sw1a, www.royalcollection.org.uk, t: 02077667300, changing of the guard apr-aug daily 11:30am, sep-mar odd days 11:30, free to view, royal state rooms entrance £20.50, tube victoria/green park/hyde park corner

⑨ Until recently the Royal Collection of the Queen's art was not open to the public. Visit the **Queen's Gallery** to see important pieces from this vast collection by artists such as Michelangelo, Vermeer, and Rubens.

buckingham palace, st. james's park, sw1a, www.royalcollection.org.uk, t: 02077667301, open daily jan-jul & oct-dec 10am-5:30pm, aug-sep 9:30am-5:30pm, entrance £10, tube victioria/green park/hyde park corner

⑩ Curious about the royal family's horses, carriages, and motor vehicles? See them for yourself at the **Royal Mews.** Here you'll find the Gold State Coach, which was built in 1762 for George III, among other artifacts.

buckingham palace, buckingham palace road, sw1w, www.royalcollection.org.uk, t: 02077667302, open daily feb-mar 10am-4pm, apr-oct 10am-5pm, closed during state visits, entrance £9, tube victoria

⑫ During the Second World War Churchill directed numerous military operations from within the subterranean **Cabinet War Rooms.** The underground complex remains virtually unchanged today and gives an excellent glimpse into life in wartime London.

king charles street, sw1a, cwr.iwm.org.uk, t: 02079306961, open daily 9:30am-6pm, entrance £18, tube westminster/st. james's park

⑬ London's best-known address, **10 Downing Street,** has been the home and office of the British Prime Minister since 1732. Many a famous foot has crossed the threshold of this notable building. Unfortunately, most of us will have to settle for a peek of the famed front door from the other side of a fence, although a virtual tour is available online.

10 downing street, sw1a, www.number10.gov.uk, tube westminster/st. james's park

⑭ **Banqueting House** is the only remaining building from the original Whitehall Palace, which burned down in 1689. Check out Rubens' stunning ceiling painting, which dates back to 1629. Fantastic classical concerts are also organized here.

whitehall, sw1a, www.hrp.org.uk/banquetinghouse, t: 08444827777, open daily 10am-5pm, entrance £6.60, tube westminster/embankment/charing cross

(15) **Horse Guards** stand watch by the official entrance to the royal palaces. The guards—both on horseback and on foot—don't appear to be keeping an eye on anything in particular. Mostly they stoically ignore the many tourists. The Changing of the Guard takes place here with all the necessary pomp and ceremony.
whitehall, sw1, www.royal.gov.uk, changing of the guard mon-sat 11am, sun 10am, free entrance, tube westminster/st. james's park/embankment

(16) **Trafalgar Square** is London's central square. People come here to protest, ring in the New Year, celebrate Eid-al-Fitr, Diwali, and the Chinese New Year, and much more. This is also a place people come to just hang out or cool off in the fountains. There is some event happening here nearly every weekend.
trafalgar square, sw1, www.london.gov.uk/trafalgarsquare, tube charing cross

(17) With tens of thousands of portraits, the **National Portrait Gallery** provides a good overview of British history from the 16th century to the present. Nearly every significant UK figure is represented here in a painting, photo, or sculpture, from Shakespeare to Kate Moss and David Bowie. The restaurant on the top floor offers a fantastic view and delicious food.
st. martin's place, wc2h, www.npg.org.uk, t: 02073060055, open mon-wed 10am-6pm, thu-fri 10am-9pm, sat-sun 10am-6pm, free entrance, tube charing cross/leicester square/embankment

(18) Unless you have several days to spend at the **National Gallery,** you'll have to make some serious choices here—you won't be able to see everything in one visit. The museum houses the national collection of Western European art from the 13th to early 20th century and includes works from Van Gogh, Monet, Seurat, Constable, and Turner.
trafalgar square, wc2n, www.nationalgallery.org.uk, t: 02077472885, open mon-thu & sat-sun 10am-6pm, fri 10am-9pm, free entrance, tube charing cross/leicester square

(24) The **Royal Academy** was Britain's first official art school and is primarily known for its temporary exhibitions. The Summer Exhibition, which showcases artwork from both established and emerging artists, is especially popular.
burlington house, piccadilly, w1j, www.royalacademy.org.uk, t: 02073008000, open daily 10am-6pm, entrance £10, tube green park/piccadilly circus

FOOD & DRINK

⑥ In one of the ancient cellars of Westminster Abbey sits **Cellarium Café & Terrace.** This charming restaurant is a nice spot for breakfast or lunch. Or try the afternoon tea, which includes sweet and savory scones and a selection of delicious cakes. The terrace is great when the weather is nice.

20 dean's yard, sw1p, www.cellariumcafe.com, t: 02072220516, open mon-fri 8am-6pm, sat 9am-5pm, sun 10am-4pm, price £8, afternoon tea £16, tube westminster/ st. james's park

⑪ **Inn the Park** is a beautiful glass-and-wood structure tucked away amid the greenery of St. James's Park. The restaurant is a great place for a delicious breakfast, lunch, or dinner and offers a picturesque view of the pond. For a romantic picnic in the park, order a basket complete with champagne, a wool blanket, and nice dishes.

st. james's park, sw1a, www.innthepark.com, t: 02074519999, open mon-fri 8am-11pm, sat-sun 9am-11pm, price £16, tube st. james's park/green park/charing cross

⑲ The upscale Haymarket Hotel is more than just a place to sleep: It also has a great bar and restaurant where you can have a nice drink or meal. **Brumus** is characterized by the same colorful style the rest of the hotel is known for and does a fabulous afternoon tea.

1 suffolk place, sw1y, www.firmdale.com, t: 02074704007, open mon-sat 7am-midnight, sun 8am-11pm, price afternoon tea from £25, tube leicester square/ piccadilly circus

㉑ Breakfast has taken on something of a cult status in London. This can be partly attributed to the epic breakfast menu at **The Wolseley,** which ranges from a simple pink grapefruit to an extravagant caviar omelet. Of course, you can also opt for something more standard like regular scrambled eggs. The Wolseley is located in a former Bentley showroom and is the perfect spot to dine in style at any time of day.

160 piccadilly, w1j, www.thewolseley.com, t: 02074996996, open mon-fri 7am-midnight, sat 8am-midnight, sun 8am-11pm, price breakfast £10, tube green park

(28) **Momo** has been fully booked night after night for almost 15 years. The cocktails here are popular, as is the delicious North African food and lively atmosphere. The weekend brunch here is also stellar. The restaurant is a vibrant oasis hidden just behind the bustling Regent Street.

25 heddon street, w1b, www.momoresto.com, t: 02074344040, open mon-fri noon-1am, sat 11am-1am, sun 11am-midnight, price £25, tube piccadilly circus/oxford circus

(29) Momo's Mourad Mazouz has taken dining out in London to a whole new level with **Sketch.** Afternoon tea in the Parlour includes bite-sized edible treasures served on funky dishes. The Gallery is an ultra-hip monochromatic space where you can enjoy delicious modern fare. Also consider the upscale Lecture Room & Library, which has two Michelin stars, and the East Bar, which is a great place for a drink. Whichever you choose, you are in for an unforgettable night out.

9 conduit street, w1s, www.sketch.uk.com, t: 02076594500, the parlour open mon-fri 8am-2am, sat 10am-2am, price the parlour £15, tube oxford circus

(31) **28°-50° Wine Workshop & Kitchen** is an excellent place to come for all things wine related, whether a simple glass, a wine tasting, or a full meal. The atmosphere here is always pleasant and, with a selection of more than 30 wines, there's sure to be something to accommodate every wine lover's palate. The restaurant offers regular wine tastings and themed wine dinners.

17-19 maddox street, w1s, www.2850.co.uk, t: 02074951505, open mon-wed noon-11pm, thu-sat noon-midnight, price £20, tube oxford circus

(33) **Mews of Mayfair** is a stylish restaurant hidden away in a small alley off the bustling New Bond Street. Start with a drink at the cocktail bar on the ground floor. Then head upstairs to the brasserie, where you can enjoy nice seafood or steak. Finally, top it all off with a relaxing after-dinner drink in the sophisticated basement lounge.

10-11 lancashire court, new bond street, w1s, www.mewsofmayfair.com, t: 02075189388, open mon-sat noon-1am, price £20, tube bond street/oxford circus

(34) Afternoon tea in the Art Deco **Claridge's** hotel is an experience like no other. The live piano and violin music, jacket-clad wait staff, clinking silver, signature

China, extensive tea selection, and delicate pastries and finger sandwiches make Claridge's the number-one place to go for a fancy afternoon tea. Reservations are required and a jacket and tie recommended.

brook street, w1, www.claridges.co.uk, t: 02076298860, afternoon tea daily 2:45pm, 3pm, 3:15pm, 3:30pm, 4:45pm, 5pm, 5:15pm & 5:30pm, price £55, tube bond street

SHOPPING

⑳ Designer Rei Kawakubo of Comme des Garçons created an entirely new type of store with **Dover Street Market.** Although not actually a market, this one-of-a-kind department store is London's top destination for cutting-edge fashion. When you need a break from shopping, head up to Rose Bakery on the top floor—the carrot cake is phenomenal!

18-22 haymarket, sw1y, www.doverstreetmarket.com, t: 02075180680, open mon-fri 11am-7pm, sat noon-5pm, tube green park

㉒ **Wolf & Badger** offers a great selection of fashion from independent, emerging designers. In addition to clothing, they also have a nice assortment of bags, shoes, jewelry, and home wares. Be sure to peek downstairs, where you can check out their music, fashion, and art installations.

32 dover street, w1s, www.wolfandbadger.com, t: 02072294848, open mon-wed 11am-6:30pm, thu-sat 11am-7pm, sun noon-5pm, tube green park

㉓ Get a taste of old England at the **Fortnum & Mason** department store. You could easily fill suitcases with all of the specialty foods here. There are also numerous restaurants at Fortnum's, including the Diamond Jubilee Tea Salon, where they offer a nice afternoon tea. Don't forget to check out the gorgeous window displays, which are especially fabulous around Christmastime.

181 piccadilly, w1a, www.fortnumandmason.com, t: 02077348040, open mon-sat 10am-9pm, sun noon-6pm, tube green park/piccadilly circus

㉕ **Burlington Arcade** is an upscale shopping arcade dating back to the 19th century. Today it's home to shops such as Penhaligon's, where you can get fragrant perfumes, and Ladurée, known for their delicious French macarons.

While shopping, be sure to look up and take in the gorgeous architecture. Watch out for the beadles—these officers, who have been patrolling the arcade since 1819, are part of the old-school charm here and won't hesitate to stop you if they catch you running, whistling, or chewing gum.

51 piccadilly, w1j, www.burlington-arcade.co.uk, t: 02074931764, open mon-sat 9am-7:30pm, sun 11am-6pm, tube green park/piccadilly circus

㉖ Both Jermyn Street and **Savile Row** are famous for their tailor-made clothing. The latter is less old fashioned, but certainly no less pricey. If you're looking for the same quality on a lower budget, go to Cad & The Dandy.

savile row, w1, open mon-sat 10am-6pm, tube oxford circus/piccadilly circus

㉗ **Regent Street** is a charming London shopping street, and Hamleys, Burberry, and & Other Stories are particularly worth a visit. Hamleys is a giant toy store, Burberry an English classic, and & Other Stories is H&M's trendy sister store where you'll find an eclectic and affordable collection of clothes, accessories, and cosmetics.

regent street, w1, www.regentstreetonline.com, open daily, tube oxford circus/ piccadilly circus

㉚ **Liberty** is many Londoners' favorite department store, not only because of the great selection here, but also thanks to the atmosphere and the beautiful Tudor-style building. It dates from 1924 and was built with the wood of two warships. You'll find everything under one roof here, including clothes, accessories, cosmetics, furniture, office supplies, and the famous Liberty fabrics.

regent street, w1b, www.liberty.co.uk, t: 02077341234, open mon-sat 10am-8pm, sun noon-6pm, tube oxford circus

㉜ Old and New **Bond Street** are the number-one shopping streets for fanatics of big-name brands. Burberry, Mulberry, Nicole Farhi, Chanel, Louis Vuitton, Gucci, and Prada all have gorgeous shops here. During the January and July sales, prices drop by more than half. Of course, then everything is so last season.

old and new bond street, w1, www.bondstreetassociation.com, t: 02078215230, open mon-sat 10am-7pm, sun noon-6pm, tube bond street/oxford circus

㉟ Those who love antiques, ceramics, silver, vintage fashion, watches, gems, and jewelry can spend hours wandering through the covered labyrinth that is **Grays Antique Market.** Over 200 vendors spread out over two buildings—Grays and the Mews—come here to sell their wares.

58 davies street & 1-7 davies mews, w1k, www.graysantiques.com,
t: 02076297034, open mon-fri 10am-6pm, sat 11am-5pm, tube bond street

㊱ Hidden behind the busy Oxford Street lies **South Molton Street.** On this charming shopping street you'll find a nice mix of jewelry, clothing, and shoe stores. European brands such as Sandro, Reiss, Kooples, Kurt Geiger, and Petit Bateau all have stores here.

south molton street, w1s, www.thelanesofmayfair.com, open daily, tube bond street

MORE TO EXPLORE

① When the **London Eye,** also known as the Millennium Wheel, opened on December 31st, 1999, it was the largest Ferris wheel in the world. It is still the tallest in Europe, and the most popular paid tourist attraction in the United King-dom. A ride lasts about half an hour and will carry you up to 443 feet in the air. On clear days, the view over London and far out into the surrounding area is breathtaking. Be sure to book a ticket in advance if you don't want to stand in line. It's also cheaper.

south bank, se1, www.londoneye.com, t: 08717813000, open daily, price tickets
from £23, tube westminster/waterloo

③ Experience British politics during Question Time in the **House of Commons.** It's a lively sight that often culminates in political theater. Only UK residents can reserve tickets ahead of time; tourists have to wait and see if there are any spots left over. The lines for Question Time can be very long, but they often move quickly for other debates.

houses of parliament, parliament square, sw1, www.parliament.uk, t: 02072194272,
open mon & tue 2:30pm-10:30pm, wed 11:30am-7:30pm, thu 10:30am-6:30pm, fri
9:30am-3pm, free entrance, tube westminster

⑦ **St. James's Park** is one of London's most beautiful green spaces. Rent a deck chair, hang out, and enjoy the fantastic view of Buckingham Palace. Bring some nuts to feed the squirrels and marvel at the pelicans swimming around.
st. james's park, sw1a, www.royalparks.org.uk, t: 03000612000, open daily 5am-midnight, free entrance, tube st. james's park/westminster

WALK 2

SOUTHWARK

ABOUT THE WALK

This varied walk takes you past historical attractions such as Tower Bridge, City Hall, and St. Paul's Cathedral. This walk focuses strongly on history and culture, and you'll pass by great museums such as Tate Modern and the Design Museum. There are plenty of restaurants, gastropubs, and charming cafés where you can get a nice bite to eat.

THE NEIGHBORHOODS

South of the Thames lies Southwark. Compared to the north side of London, this side is somewhat underappreciated. Here posh London gives way to a raw, industrial vibe with warehouses and old train overpasses. The further south you go, the shabbier the streets are. Yet there are plenty of things to see on this Southwark walk, including the **Tower of London, Tower Bridge, Tate Modern, City Hall,** and **Southwark Cathedral.** London's first theaters appeared in this neighborhood in the 16th century, including **The Globe,** where Shakespeare's first performances were held. The reconstructed theater is a popular attraction to this day. The old **Borough Market,** also on the south side of the Thames, is an absolute must for anyone who loves food.

Directly across the water stands another London icon: **St. Paul's Cathedral.** It is surrounded by **"The City,"** London's financial center (also called the Square Mile). This is the commercial pulse of London and is home to many banks and offices.

Further to the north you'll find Clerkenwell, a historical neighborhood in the center of the city. During the 12th century, this neighborhood was home to many monasteries. However, during the Industrial Revolution the area was built up and Clerkenwell transformed into a neighborhood full of factories and storehouses. The primary residents were blue-collar workers and immigrants, and for a long time the area was unsavory and dirty. In the 1980s the neighborhood was re-vived and the warehouses and historical buildings were renovated. Media companies moved in and the area's image changed. Clerkenwell is now a trendy, creative neighborhood known especially for its restaurants. There are many good restaurants and gastropubs to be found around Farringdon and **Exmouth Market** in particular.

SHORT ON TIME? HERE ARE THE HIGHLIGHTS
+ TOWER BRIDGE + BOROUGH MARKET + TATE MODERN
+ BARBICAN CENTRE + EXMOUTH MARKET

TIPS
// A varied walk, great for experienced London visitors
// The markets and restaurants make this walk perfect for foodies
// Not suitable for biking due to traffic

SIGHTS & ATTRACTIONS

① In 1066 William the Conqueror commissioned the building of the **Tower of London,** one of the last medieval castles in the world and the site of murders, executions, conspiracies, and betrayals. Discover the history and admire the extensive collection of crown jewels.

tower hill, ec3, www.hrp.org.uk/toweroflondon, t: 02031666000, open mar-oct tue-sat 9am-5:30pm, sun-mon 10am-5:30pm, nov-feb tue-sat 9am-4:30pm, sun-mon 10am-4:30pm, entrance £24.50, tube tower hill

③ The steel-framed design of **Tower Bridge** was revolutionary when it opened in 1894. Now, together with Big Ben, it is one of London's most iconic structures, not to mention one of the most famous bridges in the world. Check out the Tower Bridge Exhibition and visit the Engine Rooms inside, then traverse the high-level walkway. The view from the walkway was made even more amazing in 2014: Now you can look down through a glass panel in the floor and see what's going on 138 feet below.

tower hill, ec3, www.towerbridge.org.uk, t: 02074033761, open daily apr-sep 10am-5:30pm, oct-mar 9:30am-5pm, entrance £9, tube tower hill

⑥ The building that houses the **Fashion and Textile Museum** is hard to miss. With its outrageous color scheme of hot pink, burnt orange, yellow, and bright blue, the converted warehouse has become a tourist attraction in its own right. The museum was founded by the English fashion designer Zandra Rhodes and has regular exhibitions on fashion, textiles, and jewelry.

83 bermondsey street, se1, www.ftmlondon.org, t: 02074078664, open tue-wed & fri-sat 11am-6pm, thu 11am-8pm, sun 11am-5pm, entrance £8.80, tube london bridge

⑦ In 2002, the mayor of London got a brand-new office: **City Hall.** It's an impressive glass structure referred to by locals as the "leaning tower of pizzas" because of its tilted egg-like shape. Visit the council chambers and enjoy the view. In front of the building you'll find the Scoop, an open-air amphitheater with free music and theater performances in the summer.

the queen's walk, se1, www.london.gov.uk/city-hall, t: 02079834000, open mon-thu 8:30am-6pm, fri 8:30am-5:30pm, free entrance, tube london bridge

⑧ **Southwark Cathedral** was built during the 13th century. It's nothing short of a miracle that England's oldest cathedral still stands today, right next to a busy bridge and railroad tracks. You can hear beautiful choral music several times a week and there are daily masses. The churchyard is a wonderful place to sit and relax.

london bridge, se1, www.cathedral.southwark.anglican.org, t: 02073676700, open mon-fri 8am-6pm, sat-sun 8:30am-6pm, free entrance, price tour £5, tube london bridge

⑮ Works from most of the best-known artists from the 20th century are exhibited in the **Tate Modern,** London's museum of modern art. The impressive building—previously a power plant—is worth a visit in and of itself. A large-scale installation by a different artist is on display every year in Turbine Hall. The restaurant on the top floor is a welcome respite with a grand view out over the Thames. Be sure to check out the museum store.

bankside, se1, www.tate.org.uk, t: 02078878888, open sun-thu 10am-6pm, fri-sat 10am-10pm, free entrance, prices vary for special exhibitions, tube southwark/st. paul's/mansion house

⑯ The first pedestrian bridge over the Thames, **Millennium Bridge,** closed just three days after it opened in 2000 because it began to shake when too many people were on it. That earned it the nickname "the Wobbly Bridge." The problem has since been fixed and the bridge now offers the perfect way to cross between the Tate Modern and St. Paul's Cathedral.

tube southwark/st. paul's

⑰ **St. Paul's Cathedral** really stands out with its enormous dome. The cathedral, where Charles and Diana were married, was designed by British scientist and architect Christopher Wren, and built in the late 17th century. Climb the 521 steps for a beautiful view of London.

st. paul's churchyard, ec4m, www.stpauls.co.uk, t: 02072468357, open mon-sat 8:30am-4pm, entrance £18, tube st. paul's

⑱ The **Museum of London** recounts the story of London from prehistory to the present. See artwork, drawings, and archeological discoveries and learn more about the history of this fascinating city. You'll get answers to questions such as,

"Who was Jack the Ripper?" and, "What happened during the Great Fire of London in 1666?"

150 london wall, ec2y, www.museumoflondon.org.uk, t: 02070019844, open daily 10am-6pm, free entrance, tube barbican/st. paul's

⑲ The **Barbican Centre** is the largest multidisciplinary art center in all of Europe. Various media can be found under one roof here, from art and music to dance, theater, and film. For a little break, head to the Barbican Foodhall or the Barbican Lounge.

silk street, ec2y, www.barbican.org.uk, t: 02076388891, open mon-sat 9am-11pm, sun 11am-11pm, tube barbican

⑳ **St. Bartholomew the Great** is a gorgeous 12th-century church. This charming church has been the set of various films, including *Four Weddings and a Funeral* and *The Other Boleyn Girl*. Pay attention to the beautiful Tudor gatehouse as you enter.

west smithfield, ec1a, www.greatstbarts.com, t: 02076065171, open mon-fri 8:30am-5pm, sat 10:30am-4pm, sun 8:30am-8pm, entrance £4, tube barbican

FOOD & DRINK

⑤ For culinary inspiration and an overall good time, head to **Maltby Street Market.** This market has two main parts: Ropewalk, the street vendors, and Spa Terminus, the shops under the tracks. Stroll along the various stalls and shops, taste handmade treats, and enjoy the atmosphere.

maltby street, se1, www.maltby.st, open sat 9am-4pm, sun 11am-4pm, tube london bridge

⑩ For delicious seafood, the charming **Wright Brothers Oyster & Porter House** is the place to go. Make like a local and order a dozen oysters and a pint of Guinness—heavenly!

11 stoney street, se1, www.thewrightbrothers.co.uk/restaurant/borough-market/, t: 02074039554, open mon-fri noon-11pm, sat noon-10pm, sun noon-9pm, price from £16/half-dozen oysters, tube london bridge

(11) Sunday roast is a traditional British meal that includes meat, potatoes, and roasted vegetables. **Roast,** located above the market hall, is the perfect place to enjoy this meal. All dishes are made with fresh, local ingredients. This is also a great spot for breakfast.

the floral hall, stoney street, se1, www.roast-restaurant.com, t: 08450347300, open mon-wed 7am-midnight, thu-fri 7am-12:45am, sat 8:30am-12:45am, sun 11:30am-7:45pm, price £20, tube london bridge

(12) Monmouth coffee beans are well known in London, and there's no better place to go for a caffeine break than **Monmouth Coffee.** It feels just like your living room, but with a view out over the market and bins full of coffee beans. You can also get delicious baguettes, croissants, and cakes here.

2 park street, se1, www.monmouthcoffee.co.uk, t: 02072323010, open mon-sat 7:30am-6pm, price coffee £2.50, tube london bridge

(21) **The Old Red Cow** is a great place for a beer. This charming pub offers a large selection of beers from England, Germany, the US, and Austria. It also has a variety of ciders. If all that beer makes you hungry, order a hamburger, club sandwich, or shepherd's pie.

71-72 long lane, ec1a, www.theoldredcow.com, t: 02077262595, open mon-thu noon-11pm, fri-sat noon-midnight, sun noon-11pm, price £5, tube farringdon

(23) You'll probably have to wait for a table because **Polpo Smithfield** doesn't take reservations. The wait can be long, but once you're seated you can choose from a variety of delicious Italian classics, such as spaghetti and meatballs, linguine *vongole* (with clams), risotto and, of course, pizza.

3 cowcross street, ec1m, www.polpo.co.uk, t: 02072500034, open mon-sat noon-11pm, sun noon-4pm, price £8, tube farringdon

(24) If you're planning on eating at **Hix Oyster & Chop House,** you'd better set aside a few hours, because the food here is pure pleasure. The oysters and steak are perfect, and the ambiance is simple and stylish. Reservations are recommended.

36-37 greenhill rents, cowcross street, ec1m, www.hixoysterandchophouse.co.uk, t: 02070171930, open sun-fri noon-11pm, sat 5pm-11pm, price £18, tube farringdon

㉕ At **Burger & Lobster,** choose either a hamburger or half a lobster with fries and a salad. You can expect something more sophisticated than your regular backyard burger here. The Beast Burger is the ultimate surf and turf: A burger topped with lobster meat. Their wild Canadian lobsters are imported live from Nova Scotia. The interior is a modern, industrial take on the classic American diner.

40 st. john street, ec1m, www.burgerandlobster.com, t: 02074909230, open mon-thu noon-10:30pm, fri noon-11pm, sat 4pm-10:30pm, price £20, tube farringdon

㉖ Hidden down a small street between Clerkenwell Road and Great Sutton Street in a former diamond-cutting factory is **J+A Café.** This is a great spot for delicious breakfast, lunch, or brunch. The menu features healthy, wholesome home cooking, from simple recipes using locally sourced produce. There is always fresh-baked soda bread, a big pot of tea, and a cake on the table. The bar upstairs is nice for drinks.

1-4 sutton lane, ec1m, www.jandacafe.com, t: 02074902992, open mon-tue 8am-6pm, wed-fri 8am-11pm, sat 9am-5pm, price £5, tube barbican

㉘ Breakfast, brunch, lunch, dinner, or drinks: Anything is possible at **The Modern Pantry,** a café, restaurant, and deli all in one. Chef and owner Anna Hansen is known for her New Zealand-inspired fusion cuisine: Original flavors and dishes that combine seasonal western ingredients with the freshness and spice of Asian and Pacific Rim cooking. Sit downstairs, upstairs, or outside. This spot is particularly popular on the weekend for brunch, so it's best to make reservations.

47-48 st john's square, ec1v, www.themodernpantry.co.uk, t: 02075539210, open mon 8am-10pm, tue-fri 8am-10:30pm, sat 9am-10:30pm, sun 10am-10pm, price £12, tube farringdon

㉙ Do you love Asian cuisine? Try **KIN,** a restaurant with a minimalist interior where you can order simple yet interesting dishes from all over Asia. Try the Thai curry, Indonesian *nasi goreng* (fried rice), or the Japanese noodles.

88 leather lane, ec1n, www.kinstreetfood.com, t: 02074300886, open mon-fri noon-3pm & 5:30pm-10:30pm, sat 5:30pm-10:30pm, price £7, tube farringdon/chancery lane

FACEBOOK THECHEESETRUCK
TWITTER CHEESETRUCKLDN
INSTAGRAM THECHEESETRUCK

CITY OF LONDON

㉛ The mix of Spanish and North African fare at **Moro** is exciting, subtle, and perfect in all its simplicity. Those who are familiar with the Moro cookbook will definitely want to reserve a table here, while those who haven't yet become acquainted with the book will want to do so after eating here. Husband and wife Sam and Sam Clark share their love of food and exotic spices through dishes cooked on a charcoal grill or in a woodburning oven.

34-36 exmouth market, ec1r, www.moro.co.uk, t: 02078338336, open mon-sat noon-10:30pm, sun noon-2:45pm, price £15, tube farringdon

㉝ **Sweet** is a bakery with a small seating area. Not only do they sell the most delicious baked goods, but they also serve sandwiches and salads. This is the ideal spot for a quick bite or to quell a hankering for something sweet. But be warned: It may be difficult to resist trying more than one treat.

64a exmouth market, ec1r, www.sweetdesserts.co.uk, t: 02077136777, open mon-sat 7am-5:30pm, sun 8am-5:30pm, price £6, tube farringdon

SHOPPING

⑬ The cheeses at **Neal's Yard Dairy** come from the British Isles and are served in London's top restaurants. Pick a few delicious cheeses to enjoy at home. The staff is determined to help you find just the right type to suit your palate, even if it requires lots of sampling to do so.

6 park street, borough market, se1, www.nealsyarddairy.co.uk, t: 02073670799, open mon-sat 9am-6pm, tube london bridge

㉗ **Craft Central** has workshop spaces for designers and artists. It also occasionally opens its doors to the public, when you can buy original creations directly from the artists. Check out the website to see if your visit to London coincides with any of their events.

33-35 st. john's square, ec1m, www.craftcentral.org.uk, t: 02072510276, tube farringdon

㉚ Anyone who loves magazines and looking at beautiful pictures will surely enjoy spending some time at **Magma Bookshop.** Their selection of art, design, architecture, fashion, and music books and magazines is extensive. They also have great gift items.

117-119 clerkenwell road, ec1r, www.magmabooks.com, t: 02072429503, open mon-sat 10am-7pm, tube farringdon/chancery lane

③ **Family Tree** is a small shop with a one-of-a-kind collection of items such as fluorescent butterfly pins and exotic washi lamps. Some of the items are the store's own design, some were designed by the owner's friends, and others come from around the world.

53 exmouth market, ec1r, www.familytreeshop.co.uk, t: 02072781084, open mon-sat 11am-6pm, tube farringdon

MORE TO EXPLORE

② The **St. Katharine Docks** marina is directly next to the City. You'll see businessmen and -women in perfectly tailored suits pop over here for a quick lunch. The marina is a little slice of calm next to the bustling area around Tower Bridge and is perhaps one of the best-kept secrets in London. Different events are held here regularly, such as open air tea dance parties and a world food market every Friday from 11am to 3pm.

50 st. katharine's way, e1w, www.skdocks.co.uk, t: 02072645312, tube tower hill

④ **Butler's Wharf** is the collective name of the complex of renovated warehouses, restaurants, stores, and apartment buildings on the south side of the Thames. It's nice to walk around here and sit outside at one of the restaurants with a lovely view of Tower Bridge.

shad thames, se1, tube tower hill/london bridge

⑨ **Borough Market** is one of London's biggest and oldest markets. From Wednesday to Saturday, vendors and suppliers come here from around the country to sell some of the most delicious items: Fruits and vegetables, fish on ice, freshly made bread, chocolate, meat, jam, olives, and so much more.

borough market, se1, www.boroughmarket.org.uk, t: 02074071002, open wed-thu 10am-5pm, fri 10am-6pm, sat 8am-5pm, tube london bridge

⑭ **Shakespeare's Globe Theatre** is a reconstruction of the original theater where many of Shakespeare's best-known plays were first performed. There are performances here from April to October. The experience is just as it would have been during Shakespeare's time: Either standing in the open air or sitting on wooden benches. Tours run year-round.

21 new globe walk, bankside, se1, www.shakespearesglobe.com, t: 02074019919, open daily, see website for times, price performances from £15 (standing tickets £5), tour and exhibition £15, tube southwark/st. paul's

㉒ Meat has been bought and sold at **Smithfield Market** for the past 800 years. The beautiful Victorian building dates from 1867. If you want to see the market in full swing, you'd better get here early, preferably before 7am.

charterhouse street, ec1a, www.smithfieldmarket.com, t: 02073323092, open mon-fri 3am-noon, tube farringdon/barbican

WALK **3**

SHOREDITCH

ABOUT THE WALK

This walk takes you to the artistic part of the city. You'll go past art galleries, vintage boutiques, and creative markets. The streets around Shoreditch are interesting, and for those wanting to explore more, you can also deviate from the route and head further into East London. This is also a great place for a night out.

THE NEIGHBORHOODS

Shoreditch is in the **East End,** which was traditionally the working-class part of the city. However, with the arrival of artists and the creative sector in the late 1980s, Shoreditch was transformed into one of the hippest neighborhoods in London. There are more artists per square mile here than in any other part of Europe. Controversial artwork and the latest trends all find their beginnings in Shoreditch. Although rents have continued to rise, the artsy vibe has remained. You'll see this in all the **street art,** including the graffiti-covered walls and in-dustrial warehouses that are home to creative Web companies. Large chains are slowly taking over the neighborhood, pushing the true trendsetters farther east, toward up-and-coming neighborhoods such as Dalston and Stoke Newington.

Shoreditch is not only popular for its creative vibe, but also for its nightlife. Clubs, pubs, restaurants, markets, and coffee shops—this area has it all. The neighbor-hood is also home to Asian and other international communities that contribute to making this artistic melting pot a fascinating place. It has famous streets such as **Brick Lane,** also known as Banglatown. Londoners come here for the only true national dish: curry!

One of the most notorious East Enders is the serial killer Jack the Ripper. Around 1888, he assaulted and killed numerous prostitutes in and near Shoreditch. These so-called Whitechapel murders have been the inspiration for over 100 novels, poems, comic books, games, songs, plays, operas, television programs, and films. Who exactly Jack the Ripper was and why he did it remains a mystery to this day. There are many rumors and stories floating around that keep this story alive.

SHORT ON TIME? HERE ARE THE HIGHLIGHTS
+ WHITECHAPEL GALLERY + SUNDAY UPMARKET + BOXPARK SHOREDITCH + GEFFRYE MUSEUM + BRICK LANE

TIPS
// This is a young, hip, and creative neighborhood
// Good for a Sunday walk, thanks to all the markets
// A great spot to experience London nightlife

SIGHTS & ATTRACTIONS

① For innovative contemporary art exhibitions, there is no better place in London than **Whitechapel Gallery.** Exhibitions change regularly and there are often interesting readings here. It may not be as well-known as the Tate Modern, but it is certainly just as rewarding.

77-82 whitechapel high street, e1, www.whitechapelgallery.org, t: 02075227888, open tue-wed & fri-sun 11am-6pm, thu 11am-9pm, free entrance, tube aldgate east

㉜ The **Geffrye Museum** offers a unique look into the life of Londoners and the interiors of their homes. You'll see an overview of the various interior styles in middle-class English homes from 1600 to the present. The gorgeously kept gardens are also worth a visit.

136 kingsland road, e2, www.geffrye-museum.org.uk, t: 02077399893, open tue-sun 10am-5pm, free entrance, overground hoxton

FOOD & DRINK

⑩ Chocolate lovers might want to keep walking, because it is difficult to resist the temptations at **Dark Sugars.** Chocolate truffles are displayed here alongside an assortment of chocolate bonbons, all with unusual flavor combinations. Try flavors such as ginger and honey, cardamom, cognac, or coffee and walnut.

141 brick lane, e1, facebook: darksugarschocolates, open mon-sat 11am-7pm, overground shoreditch high street

⑪ *Fika* is a Swedish expression that refers to a coffee break, but it also means having nice food and drinks in good company. **Fika Bar & Kitchen** is open from early in the morning until late at night. Come here for breakfast, lunch, afternoon coffee, or dinner. It's not fancy, but the food is delicious. The décor is Scandinavian and the food includes Swedish meatballs, salmon, and *kladdkada,* a gooey chocolate cake served with vanilla ice cream.

161 brick lane, e1, www.fikalondon.com, t: 02076132013, open mon-thu noon-11pm, fri noon-midnight, sat 10am-midnight, sun 10am-10:30pm, price £10, overground shoreditch high street

⑫ Pizza fans take note. **Story** makes exceptional fresh pizzas using organic ingredients. This is a favorite spot among Shoreditch residents and workers.
123 bethnal green road, e2, www.storydeli.com, t: 07918197352, open daily noon-10:30pm, price £18, overground shoreditch high street

⑮ **Rochelle Canteen** is the in-crowd's little secret, so mum's the word. This restaurant is only open during the week and is difficult to find. Ring the bell that says "canteen" at the boys' entrance to this former school. A culinary adventure awaits you. The restaurant, located in the old bike shed, serves up a daily menu of British fare with a twist.
rochelle school, arnold circus, e2, www.arnoldandhenderson.com, t: 02077295667, open mon-fri 9am-4:30pm, price £10, tube shoreditch high street/old street

⑰ Order from a selection of delicious sandwiches, cakes, and pastries at **The Lily Vanilli Bakery,** then bring your food to one of the wooden tables inside or in the charming courtyard to enjoy. This is definitely the place to come if you're in the mood for a cup of tea and something yummy. But it's only open on Sunday.
6 the courtyard, ezra street, e2, www.lilyvanilli.com, open sun 8:30am-4pm, overground hoxton

⑱ In the basement of the Boundary hotel sits the eponymous restaurant, and upstairs is a great rooftop bar. Yet the biggest attraction here is undoubtedly the café and bakery, **Albion.** Come here for an early breakfast, a late dinner, or at any moment in between. The menu is full of British favorites and the food is always delicious.
2-4 boundary street, e2, www.albioncaff.co.uk, t: 02077291051, open sun-wed 8am-11pm, thu-sat 8am-1am, price £10, overground shoreditch high street

⑳ Peruvian cuisine has long been a hit in London. **Andina** is a colorful restaurant where you can get classic Peruvian dishes such as *ceviche:* Raw fish marinated in "tiger's milk." During the day, come here for breakfast or lunch with fresh-pressed Peruvian juice, and at night enjoy a variety of *ceviches* and cocktails.
1 redchurch street, e2, www.andinalondon.com, t: 02079206499, open mon-fri 8am-11pm, sat-sun 10am-11pm, price £9, overground shoreditch high street

㉒ Where you see the giant letters *T-E-A* up on the roof, you'll know you've found **Pizza East.** The big, industrial space makes it less than ideal for an intimate dinner with your date, but perfect for a fun night out with friends. On weekends this is also a popular spot for brunch. The pizzas and *antipasti* here are out of this world.

56 shoreditch high street, e1, www.pizzaeast.com, t: 02077291888, open mon-wed noon-midnight, thu noon-1am, fri noon-2am, sat 10am-2am, sun 10am-midnight, price £12, tube shoreditch high street/old street

㉕ For delicious cocktails and a lively evening, **The Hoxton Pony** is the perfect spot. The Tea Party, which includes cocktails from teapots and plates of delicious snacks, is particularly fun. Reservations are a good idea (and bring your confirmation).

104-108 curtain road, ec2a, www.thehoxtonpony.com, t: 02076132844, open tue-thu 5pm-1am, fri 5pm-2am, sat 6pm-2am, price cocktails from £8, tube shoreditch high street/old street

㉘ The **Breakfast Club** is a great place for breakfast all day long. The menu includes dishes such as scrambled eggs with salmon, pancakes with syrup, and a variety of burritos, wraps, and sandwiches. The restaurant has a nice mix of old tables and chairs, and a laidback ambiance.

2-4 rufus street, n1, www.thebreakfastclubcafes.com, t: 02077295252, open mon-wed 8am-11pm, thu-sat 8am-midnight, sun 8am-10pm, price £8, tube shoreditch high street/old street

㉙ **Rivington Bar & Grill,** a local favorite, is located in a beautiful old warehouse. They serve tasty cocktails and typical British fare in a sleek interior decorated with modern art. With a seasonal menu that features different daily specials, this is a good spot for a special occasion, or just for beer and burgers at a good price.

28-30 rivington street, ec2a, www.rivingtongrill.co.uk, t: 02077297053, open mon-fri noon-11pm, sat 10am-11pm, sun 10am-10pm, price £16, tube old street

㉚ Head to **The Book Club** for anything from an early breakfast to a late night-cap. Two floors of a former Victorian warehouse are now home to this restaurant

and bar. Fun activities are organized here as well, such as ping-pong, cabaret, and pub quizzes.

100 leonard street, ec2a, www.wearetbc.com, open mon-wed 8am-midnight, thu-fri 8am-2am, sat 10am-2am, sun 10am-midnight, price lunch £8, tube old street

SHOPPING

③ If you love vintage pieces but don't want to sort through piles of clothes to find them, **Blondie** is the place for you. The store has already done all the sorting for you (which is reflected in the price tags).

114-118 commercial street, e1, t: 02072470050, open daily 11am-7pm, tube liverpool street/aldgate east

⑤ **Rough Trade East** is a music store, coffee shop, stage, and Internet café in one. Music aficionados can spend hours here. If you're lucky, your favorite band might just be performing as you browse around.

the old truman brewery, 91 brick lane, e1, www.roughtrade.com, t: 02073927788, open mon-thu 8am-9pm, fri 8am-8pm, sat 10am-8pm, sun 11am-7pm, tube liverpool street

⑦ Those who like one-of-a-kind clothing will definitely want to check out **The Laden Showroom.** They stock clothes and accessories from dozens of independent, emerging designers. You're certain to find original items here.

103 brick lane, e1, www.laden.co.uk, t: 02072472431, open mon-fri 11am-6:30pm, sat 11am-7pm, sun 10:30am-6pm, overground shoreditch high street

⑧ **Cheshire Street** is a side street of Brick Lane and has some of the most original stores. Noteworthy spots include House of Vintage and Beyond Retro, which have fantastic vintage clothes, and Mar Mar Co, which has a variety of good-looking design items. Discover beautiful, exclusive jewelry at Comfort Station, and don't forget Duke of Uke, London's only true ukulele and banjo shop.

cheshire street, ec2, open in general mon-wed & fri-sat 10am-7pm, thu 10am-8pm, sun 11:30am-6pm, tube shoreditch high street/old street

⑨ Behind **Lik & Neon**'s fluorescent orange storefront lies a sleek interior. This tiny shop has T-shirts, CDs, newspapers, accessories, and other items, all of which are equally fun and unique.

106 sclater street, e1, www.likneon.com, t: 02077294650, open mon noon-7pm, tue-sat 11am-7pm, sun 11am-6:30pm, tube shoreditch high street/old street

⑭ Looking for nice things for your home, garden, or kitchen? At **Labour and Wait** you'll find a mix of timeless home accessories and stylish gift ideas. Odds are you won't leave here empty-handed.

85 redchurch street, e2, www.labourandwait.co.uk, t: 02077296253, open tue-sun 11am-6pm, overground shoreditch high street

⑲ The **Sunspel** brand has been around for more than 150 years and has several stores across London. Here you'll find timeless yet comfortable polos, sweaters, and underwear for men.

7 redchurch street, e2, www.sunspel.com, t: 02077399729, open mon-sat 11am-7pm, sun noon-5pm, overground shoreditch high street

㉑ What is the purpose of **Celestine Eleven**? To rejuvenate your spirit and your wardrobe with an extensive collection of fashion labels, accessories, raw food products, and beautiful coffee-table books. This is a great store to browse and pick up one-of-a-kind items.

4 holywell lane, ec2a, www.celestineeleven.com, t: 02077292987, open mon-sat 11am-7pm, sun noon-5pm, overground shoreditch high street

㉓ **Boxpark Shoreditch** is the world's first pop-up shopping center. Stacked containers have been magically transformed into stores, cafés, and galleries where you'll find fashion and lifestyle brands such as Vagabond, Filling Pieces, and Urbanears. It's a completely new shopping experience.

2-4 bethnal green road, e1, www.boxpark.co.uk, shops open mon-wed & fri-sat 11am-7pm, thu 11am-8pm, sun noon-6pm, cafés & galleries open mon-sat 8am-11pm, sun 10am-10pm, tube shoreditch high street

㉔ Javvy M. Royle and Frieda Gormley founded **House of Hackney** in 2010. This small designer department store sells only English designs, including furniture,

home accessories, clothing, textiles, wallpaper, and stationery, all covered in the most gorgeous prints.

131 shoreditch high street, e1, www.houseofhackney.com, t: 02077393901, open mon-sat 10am-7:30pm, sun 11am-5pm, overground shoreditch high street

㉖ If you love home furnishings, there will be plenty at **SCP** to add to your wish list. Items by contemporary British designers such as Terence Woodgate, Matthew Hilton, and Tom Dixon are showcased here along with classic designs by Verner Panton and Eileen Gray.

135-139 curtain road, ec2a, www.scp.co.uk, t: 02077391869, open mon-sat 9:30am-6pm, sun 11am-5pm, tube shoreditch high street/old street

㉗ Vintage clothes, shoes, and accessories for men and women are neatly displayed at **Paper Dress.** The prices here are very reasonable, especially considering the quality. If you're not sure whether to buy a certain item, think it over while enjoying a drink at the vintage bar. Live bands give regular performances here.

114-116 curtain road, ec2a, www.paperdressvintage.co.uk, t: 02077294100, open mon 10am-9pm, tue 10am-10:30pm, wed-fri 10am-11:30pm, sat 11am-11:30pm, sun noon-6pm, tube shoreditch high street/old street

MORE TO EXPLORE

② **Spitalfields Market** has been modernized in the last few years, and more big chains have moved in. And although many of these are fun to shop at, it has affected the market's unique character. Even so, stores such as Traffic People, which sells affordable designer clothes, and restaurants such as Square Pie and Smiths, which has great lunch, still make this a worthwhile place to come shop. Thursday features market stalls with antique and vintage items, and stalls on Friday display clothes and art. All of the stalls are open on Sunday, but you'll have to contend with the crowds.

105a commercial street, e1, www.oldspitalfieldsmarket.com, t: 02072478556, open mon-fri & sun 10am-5pm, sat 11am-5pm, tube liverpool street

(4) **Sunday Upmarket,** in the old Truman Brewery, is the perfect spot to buy unique handmade products directly from the designer or maker. More than 140 vendors sell clothes, art, and delicious baked goods here. The vibe is reminiscent of the Spitalfields of yesteryear.

the old truman brewery, 91 brick lane, e1, www.sundayupmarket.co.uk,
t: 02077706028, open sun 10am-5pm, tube aldgate east/liverpool street

(6) The Big Chill is an annual festival and record label that will take you back in time. The **Big Chill Bar** ensures that you can enjoy the Big Chill vibe every day. The music is usually fantastic.

dray walk, the old truman brewery, e1, wearebigchill.com, t: 02073929180, open
sun-thu noon-midnight, fri-sat noon-1am, price £8, tube liverpool street

(13) The **Electric Cinema** is a cozy movie theater that primarily screens European and arthouse films. It has 47 seats and you can choose from a variety of comfortable leather chairs, ottomans, and blankets.

64-66 redchurch street, e2, www.electriccinema.co.uk/shoreditch, t: 02033503490,
open daily noon-9:30pm, price tickets from £8, overground shoreditch high street

(16) Every Sunday Columbia Road is in full bloom with the **Columbia Road Flower Market.** This market attracts Londoners with green thumbs, but it's the shops and cafés that make it really fun. Stop by Jones Dairy for yummy bagels or Treacle for delicious cupcakes. Angela Flanders has unique perfumes, and Supernice sells hip wall stickers—and that's just for starters.

columbia road, e2, www.columbiaroad.info, market open sun 8am-3pm, tube old
street

(31) As Shoreditch continues to become increasingly gentrified, its original residents—a melting pot of immigrants, blue-collar workers, artists and other creatives—are forced to move further east in search of affordable housing. And so the hipster scene has moved eastward with them. **Broadway Market** is where the city's uber-cool flock to. This is the perfect place to sit with a cup of coffee on a Saturday morning while you watch London's trendsetters pass by. Enjoy old-fashioned jellied eel at F. Cooke. Donlon Books and Artwords sell exclusive photography and art books that you won't find anywhere else.

The Spinach & Agushi stall has the perfect chicken stew with peanut sauce. And if you already have enough clothes, handmade quilts, knickknacks, and other odds and ends, head to Off Broadway for a cocktail. The market itself has been here for many years. Historical records show that there were already vendors hawking their wares at Broadway Market in the 1890s, and Fred Cooke was known for selling his jellied eel to shepherds as far back as 1900 (today the shop is run by his grandson Bob). The vibrant street that withstood two world wars fell into decline in the 1980s, but was given a new lease on life in 2004 when local residents revived the market.

broadway market, e8, www.broadwaymarket.co.uk, open sat 9am-5pm, tube bethnal green, train london fields

WALK **4**

KING'S CROSS & ANGEL

ABOUT THE WALK

This walk will take you through two neighborhoods: King's Cross and Angel. King's Cross is changing rapidly, with new hotspots popping up left and right. Angel is not an ideal place to start your vacation if you've never been to London before—the focus here is mainly on eating, drinking, and shopping.

THE NEIGHBORHOODS

In the northern part of central London you'll find two increasingly popular neighborhoods: King's Cross and Angel.

King's Cross in particular is evolving fast. Not long ago, the neighborhood was plagued by prostitution and crime, but since the 1990s the area has undergone a significant transformation. With the arrival of the Eurostar high-speed railway service in 2007, and major renovations to the King's Cross/St. Pancras International station and the surrounding dilapidated buildings, King's Cross is now a completely different place. Not to mention famous with *Harry Potter* fans, who know that King's Cross station is where Harry catches the Hogwarts Express from Platform 9 ¾ (there's a photo op and gift shop here).

Granary Square is a great example of the recent development. This square is surrounded by renovated warehouses that are now home to cool restaurants and the famous fashion school **Central Saint Martins.** An entirely new neighborhood has gone up around Granary Square. Once all of the construction is complete, King's Cross will have some 20 new streets, 2,000 new homes, and more than 10,000 extra square feet of store, office, and living space. Google even opened its massive London headquarters here in 2016.

About a 10-minute walk to the east you'll find Islington, and at its center the charming Angel. This is a bustling neighborhood, known for **Upper Street** and

Essex Road. You won't find any big museums or tourist attractions here, but you will find a varied selection of stores, pubs, theaters, and restaurants. This neighborhood is very close to the financial center known as "The City" and the creative Clerkenwell neighborhood. It is a popular and diverse residential neighborhood where you'll find a mix of students, young families, and career-focused couples.

SHORT ON TIME? HERE ARE THE HIGHLIGHTS
**+ GRANARY SQUARE + KINGS PLACE + CAMDEN PASSAGE
+ SADLER'S WELLS + OTTOLENGHI**

TIPS
// Good route if you've been to London before
// The many restaurants and bars make this an ideal evening destination
// Recommended for theater lovers

SIGHTS & ATTRACTIONS

① With over five million visitors annually, the **British Museum** is, hands down, London's most-visited attraction. And for good reason—the collection is second to none. Here you'll find Egyptian and Asian collections, and an enormous collection of Greek and Roman art, among other treasures.

great russell street, wc1b, www.britishmuseum.org, t: 02073238299, open daily 10am-5:30pm, free entrance, tube tottenham court road/holborn

② The **Wellcome Collection** describes itself as a "destination for the incurably curious." Here, the connections between science, medicine, art, and life in the past, present, and future are explored through a unique series of contemporary and historic exhibitions and collections, public events, and digital projects. The museum is named after Sir Henry Wellcome, a famous pharmacist, philanthropist, and collector. Stop by the Wellcome Café for a cup of coffee and a yummy bite to eat.

183 euston road, nw1, www.wellcomecollection.org, t: 02076112222, open tue-wed & fri-sat 10am-6pm, thu 10am-8pm, sun 11am-6pm, free entrance, tube euston square/euston

③ With more than 150 million books, magazines, and documents in its collection, **The British Library** is one of the most expansive libraries in the world. Only members are allowed in the reading room, but there are exhibitions, events, and tours that allow you to enjoy this stately building. There is also a store, café, and restaurant.

96 euston road, nw1, www.bl.uk, t: 08432081144, open mon-thu 9:30am-8pm, fri 9:30am-6pm, sat 9:30am-5pm, sun 11am-5pm, tube king's cross/st. pancras

⑪ The **London Canal Museum** is located in a former ice house. This small museum is dedicated entirely to London's canals. Taking a boat trip is fun, and some tour boats stop here. Tours will take you over Regent's Canal and past Little Venice, London Zoo, and Camden Town.

12-13 new wharf road, n1, www.canalmuseum.org.uk, t: 02077130836, open tue-sun 10am-4:30pm, entrance £4, tube king's cross

FOOD & DRINK

④ The **Booking Office** used to sell train tickets around the year 1860. Today this historical space serves as a bar and restaurant in the St. Pancras Renaissance London Hotel. The space has high brick walls, a 95-foot-long bar, and cathedral-like elements. Enjoy a delicious breakfast, lunch, dinner, or a nice drink here.

euston road, nw1, www.bookingofficerestaurant.com, t: 02078413566, open mon-wed & sun 6:30am-1am, thu-sat 6:30am-3am, price £18, tube king's cross/st. pancras

⑤ In the newly renovated Great Northern Hotel you'll find **Plum + Spilt Milk,** an elegant restaurant where you can start the day with a nice breakfast. Evenings are lovely for drinks that can turn into a late dinner. The interior is stylish, with designer lighting and dark furniture, and the food is a modern take on British fare.

great northern hotel, pancras road, n1c, www.plumandspiltmilk.com, t: 02033880818, open mon-fri 7am-11pm, sat 8am-11pm, sun 8am-10pm, price £20, tube king's cross

⑦ Granary Square is the home base of Bruno Loubet's new restaurant, **Grain Store.** This spot is highly recommended for vegetarians, as veggies are the star ingredients on the menu. Butternut squash raviolis, artichoke paella, and freshly baked focaccia are just a few of the delicious options on the menu. Meat-eaters definitely won't be disappointed here, either. The restaurant's terrace deserves a special mention.

granary square, 1-3 stable street, n1c, www.grainstore.com, t: 02073244466, open mon-wed 10am-11:30pm, thu-sat 10am-midnight, sun 11am-4pm, price £20, tube king's cross

⑧ In a renovated warehouse on Granary Square you'll find **Caravan.** This is a favorite breakfast spot among locals, but is great any time of day. The menu includes everything from French toast and poached eggs to fresh salad and pizza. They even roast their own coffee beans.

granary building, granary square, n1c, www.caravankingscross.co.uk, t: 02071017661, open mon-tue 8am-10:30pm, wed-thu 8am-11pm, fri 8am-midnight, sat 10am-midnight, sun 10am-4pm, price £20, tube king's cross

⑨ Every Tuesday through Friday around lunchtime at Cubitt Square, a group of food trucks come together to form **Kerb Food.** You'll find Kerb at various locations throughout the city. There are different trucks every day serving up delicious burgers, tacos, falafel, and hotdogs.

cubitt square, n1c, www.kerbfood.com, open tue-fri noon-2pm, price £4, tube king's cross

⑫ **Drink, Shop & Do** is a design store, café, and overall great place to go out. Come here for an afternoon of hanging out, a spot of tea, or an evening of dancing and cocktails. The venue has a nostalgic feel thanks to the retro furniture and the cheerful use of colors. Everything here is for sale, from the artwork on the walls to the dishes, homemade cakes, and vintage furniture.

9 caledonian road, n1, www.drinkshopdo.com, t: 02072784335, open mon-thu 10:30am-midnight, fri-sat 10:30am-2am, sun 10:30am-8pm, price cocktails from £8.50, tube king's cross/st. pancras

⑬ Tucked away in a small courtyard is **Bar Pepito.** Come here to drink sherry and eat tapas in a charming interior with colorful tiles and Spanish decorations.

3 varnishers yard, the regent's quarter, www.barpepito.co.uk, t: 02078417331, open mon-fri 5pm-midnight, sat 6pm-1am, price tapas from £4, tube king's cross

⑲ As the name suggests, **The Elk in the Woods** makes you feel as though you were in a forest cabin. The interior is full of wood, deer antlers, and animal skins. Come here from early in the morning until late in the evening for a sandwich, chicken salad, or steak. Reservations are recommended.

37-39 camden passage, n1, www.the-elk-in-the-woods.co.uk, t: 02072263535, open daily 9am-11pm, price £10, tube angel

㉑ At the nameless cocktail bar known simply as **69 Colebrooke Row,** the concoctions are astonishingly good. This hole-in-the-wall is tucked away down a calm street, and if you're not paying attention you'll walk right by it. The interior feels as though you've stepped into the 1920s, and owner Tony Conigliaro mixes up cocktails with names like Death in Venice, Honeysuckle, and Spitfire.

69 colebrooke row, n1, www.69colebrookerow.com, t: 07540528593, open sun-wed 5pm-midnight, thu 5pm-1am, fri-sat 5pm-2am, price £10.50, tube angel

㉔ **Ottolenghi** is a well-known figure in London and beyond. His cookbooks are bestsellers, and he put ingredients such as pomegranate, tahini, and *za'atar* on the map. You can enjoy Mediterranean fare and copious amounts of vegetables at one of his delis and restaurants on Upper Street. Reservations are recommended.

287 upper street, n1, www.ottolenghi.co.uk, t: 02072881454, open mon-sat 8am-10:30pm, sun 9am-7pm, price £10, tube angel/highbury & islington

㉖ **Fig & Olive** is popular among Islington residents, who come here for the ambiance, the delicious food, and the excellent service. European food with a Mediterranean twist, such as *moussaka,* sea bass, and lamb, are served up in a sleek, modern interior. Come here for breakfast or a light lunch during the day.

151 upper street, n1, www.figolive.co.uk, open mon-thu 11am-11pm, fri 11am-11:30pm, sat 9am-11:30pm, sun 9am-10:30pm, price £11, tube angel/highbury & islington

㉛ Located in an old building that dates from around 1800 you'll find the charming gastropub **The Pig and Butcher.** The ambiance is inviting, the interior is warm and homey, and the food is typically English. The menu consists of local products such as vegetables and meat sourced from farmers around England. Order lamb, steak, or grilled fish, or make like a local and have a traditional Sunday roast.

80 liverpool road, n1, www.thepigandbutcher.co.uk, t: 02072268304, open mon-wed 5pm-11pm, thu 5pm-midnight, fri-sat noon-1am, sun noon-11pm, price £15, tube angel/highbury & islington

SHOPPING

⑮ **Present & Correct** is the brainchild of two graphic designers with a love of office supplies. This shop carries a collection of simple yet stylishly designed stationery and office supplies such as notebooks, paper clips, envelopes, books, prints, and postcards. This is a great spot to pick up gifts.

23 arlington way, ec1r, www.presentandcorrect.com, t: 02072782460, open tue-sat noon-6:30pm, tube angel

(17) With the arrival of famous retail chains such as Reiss, the past few years have seen significant change at **Camden Passage.** However, collectors and antique lovers can still come here every Wednesday and Saturday in search of antique and vintage objects. On other days, you can check out stores like Annie for vintage clothes, or Rockarchive Gallery for prints of rock stars.

camden passage, n1, www.camdenpassageislington.co.uk, market open wed 9am-4pm, sat 9am-5pm, tube angel

(18) Graphic and interior designer Lizzie Evans shopped in Camden Passage as a young girl. Today she has her own shop here, **Smug,** where you'll find furniture from the 1950s, handmade toys, cool kitchen accessories, and ceramics.

13 camden passage, n1, www.ifeelsmug.com, t: 02073540253, open tue & sun noon-5pm, wed & fri 11am-6pm, thu noon-7pm, sat 10am-6pm, tube angel

(20) Creative souls will undoubtedly feel like kids in a candy store at **Cass Art.** Spread out over three floors, this store has everything you could imagine when it comes to painting, drawing, and art supplies. This is a great place for artists and students, as well as anyone with a creative side. The store hosts regular workshops and readings.

66-67 colebrooke row, n1, www.cassart.co.uk, t: 02076192601, open mon-wed & fri-sat 10am-7pm, thu 10am-8pm, sun 11am-5:30pm, tube angel

(23) The brand **Aesop** was founded in 1987 and specializes in natural personal care products. Everything has been rigorously tested and is 100 percent natural. The store's minimalist interior—with white walls, wooden floors, and metal shelves—evokes a 1930s laboratory.

56 cross street, n1, www.aesop.com, t: 02071480349, open mon-sat 10am-6pm, sun noon-5pm, tube angel/highbury & islington

(25) **Albam** is a must-visit store for the fashion-conscious man. This is where local London men shop. The collection is based on trendy streetwear, including denim, fine knits, and colorful jackets with nice details. The emphasis here is on quality and the clothes are made with excellent fabrics.

286 upper street, n1, www.albamclothing.com, t: 02073541424, open mon-sat 11am-7pm, sun 11:30am-5:30pm, tube angel/highbury & islington

㉗ It may be unlikely that you'll return from a trip to London with a new sofa or dining room table, but that's no reason not to stop by **Aria.** Here you'll find original gifts and great accessories from brands such as Bodum, Cowshed, Fatboy, Ittala, and Marikmekko.

barnsbury hall, barnsbury street, n1, www.ariashop.co.uk, t: 02077046222, open mon-sat 10am-6:30pm, sun 10am-5pm, tube angel/highbury & islington

㉘ At **Folklore** you'll find furniture, lighting, art, accessories, and original gifts, all equally beautiful and well designed. The products are handmade, antique, or made from recycled material. Environmentally conscious design enthusiasts in particular will enjoy this shop.

193 upper street, n1, www.shopfolklore.com, t: 02073549333, open mon-sat 11am-6pm, sun noon-5:30pm, tube highbury & islington

㉙ Thanks to its unique mix of new and established fashion brands, **Diverse** is a great shopping spot. Acne, Helmut Lang, and Marc Jacobs are just a few of the many brands on offer. It's not cheap, but you are guaranteed to find über-on trend articles of clothing here.

294 upper street, n1, www.diverseclothing.com, t: 02073598877, open mon-wed & fri-sat 10:30am-6:30pm, thu 10:30am-7pm, sun 11:30am-5:30pm, tube angel/highbury & islington

㉚ You'll find one-of-a-kind gifts at **After Noah.** Among the old and antique furniture, postcards, and many knickknacks, you'll also find a great collection of old-fashioned toys.

121 upper street, n1, www.afternoah.com, t: 02073594281, open mon-sat 10am-6pm, sun 11am-5pm, tube angel/highbury & islington

MORE TO EXPLORE

⑥ Behind King's Cross Station you'll find **Granary Square,** a new square with spectacular fountains, consisting of 1,080 choreographed water jets. Each jet is individually controlled and lit, and together they squirt and splash in patterns. This is a great spot to hang out on a sunny day—especially with children. The renovated warehouses are now home to trendy restaurants and the university building of London's most famous fashion school, Central Saint Martins. Events and festivals are organized here year-round, including an open-air movie theater in the summer and an ice skating rink in the winter.

granary square, n1c, www.kingscross.co.uk/open-space-granary-square, tube king's cross

⑩ For classical music, art, and theater, head to **Kings Place.** This cultural center has two concert halls, several art galleries, a bar, and the Rotunda restaurant. Come here day or night for a bite to eat, or enjoy a drink outside with a view of the canal.

90 york way, n1, www.kingsplace.co.uk, t: 02075201440, open daily 9am-9pm, price tickets from £10, tube king's cross

⑭ The **Old Red Lion Theatre** is an intimate, charming theater with 60 seats and a typical English ambiance. New and classic theater productions have been staged here for more than 30 years. If you want to hang out after a performance, head to the Old Red Lion Pub for an English beer or a glass of wine.

418 st. john street, ec1v, www.oldredliontheatre.co.uk, t: 0844124307, open mon-thu noon-midnight, fri-sat noon-1am, sun noon-11pm, tube angel

⑯ **Sadler's Wells** is one of London's most historic dance theaters, with more than 300 years of history. All forms of dance can be enjoyed here, from modern and tango to hip-hop and flamenco. This is highly recommended for those who enjoy contemporary dance.

rosebery avenue, ec1r, www.sadlerswells.com, t: 02078638000, open daily, tube angel

㉒ Anyone wanting to escape the chaos of London can find respite at **Angel Therapy Rooms.** Enjoy a massage, facial, or other holistic therapy treatment in a beautiful Victorian townhouse. The treatments are not cheap, but you're guaranteed to leave this spa feeling relaxed and rejuvenated.

16b essex road, n1, www.angeltherapyrooms.com, t: 02072261188, open mon-tue noon-8pm, wed-fri 10am-8pm, sat-sun 11am-7pm, price treatments from £45, tube angel

㉜ For a great night of film, head to **The Screen on the Green.** Catch a film in this small, charming theater from the comfort of a nice armchair or loveseat. They show everything from blockbuster hits to old classics.

83 upper street, n1, www.everymancinema.com, t: 08719069060, open daily, price tickets from £12, tube angel

WALK 5

MARYLEBONE, REGENT'S PARK & PRIMROSE HILL

ABOUT THE WALK

This walk begins in the charming Marylebone neighborhood. You'll find a great selection of stores and restaurants on Marylebone High Street. The second part of the walk will take you to Regent's Park and Primrose Hill, two great places to get some fresh air either on foot or by bike. This is a long, varied walk.

THE NEIGHBORHOODS

Marylebone and Primrose Hill are two charming neighborhoods. In between you'll find Regent's Park.

Marylebone is located north of Oxford Street and is primarily home to well-heeled professionals, expats, and celebrities. This neighborhood has a quite, laid-back vibe, but with a selection of stores and restaurants that make it the envy of all others. **Marylebone High Street** and **Marylebone Lane** form the central axis of this neighborhood. There are countless fashion boutiques, restaurants, and cozy cafes in and around Marylebone High Street. Marylebone Lane is a street with even more great places to shop. It also has the best fish and chips in the city. In the 1960s, this area was a favorite of the Beatles, and both Paul McCartney and John Lennon have lived here. Other former residents include Charles Dickens, Jimi Hendrix, and fictional detective Sherlock Holmes.

North of Marylebone you'll find **Regent's Park.** This beautiful park is surrounded by stately buildings. **Primrose Hill,** a nearby residential neighborhood, is a charming hidden corner of London. The view out over the city is spectacular from the top of the hill. The small-town feel, colorful facades, and seagulls overhead make it an easygoing atmosphere. The neighborhood centers on **Regent's Park Road.** This street has a number of wonderful stores and restaurants. The odds are good that you'll see a familiar face here—the neighborhood has its share of well-known residents. In the 1990s the area was home to the Primrose Hill set, London's hippest group of friends, including Kate Moss, Jude Law, Ewan McGregor, and the Oasis brothers.

SHORT ON TIME? HERE ARE THE HIGHLIGHTS
+ MARYLEBONE HIGH STREET + THE GOLDEN HIND + REGENT'S PARK
+ THE VIEW FROM PRIMROSE HILL + REGENT'S PARK ROAD

TIPS
// A long, varied walk—
great for first-time visitors
// A perfect walk for
shopaholics
// The second half of this
walk is well-suited
for biking

SIGHTS & ATTRACTIONS

⑪ The **Wallace Collection** is not well known among the general public, which makes it all that much nicer. It is an impressive collection of 17th-century paintings, 18th-century furniture, and a variety of other art objects. Everything is exhibited in the intimate setting of the stately home in their original intended spots. The sunny courtyard is also a unique setting for a delicious afternoon tea.

manchester square, w1u, www.wallacecollection.org, t: 02075639500, open daily 10am-5pm, free entrance, tube bond street/baker street

⑳ Directly across from the famous Madame Tussauds is the gigantic underground hangar **Ambika P3.** Come here to see all types of artwork, from installations to photography, all of which is perfectly suited for display in this enormous space.

university of westminster, 35 marylebone road, nw1, www.p3exhibitions.com, t: 02079115876, open wed-fri 11am-7pm, sat-sun noon-6pm, free entrance, tube baker street

㉒ The museum at **The Royal Academy of Music** is a true pleasure for music lovers. The instruments, art objects, and sheet music on display are all still used by staff and students at the Academy. If you're lucky, your visit may coincide with an impromptu concert.

marylebone road, nw1, www.ram.ac.uk, t: 02078737373, open mon-fri 11:30am-5:30pm, sat noon-4pm, free entrance, tube baker street/regent's park

FOOD & DRINK

④ England might be known for its tea, but for a good cup of coffee, Londoners head to **Workshop Coffee.** A team of baristas roast the coffee themselves. They also offer an assortment of sandwiches, croissants, and cakes to go with your coffee.

75 wigmore street, w1u, www.workshopcoffee.com, t: 02074874902, open mon-fri 7am-7pm, sat-sun 9am-6pm, price £2, tube bond street

⑥ **Paul Rothe & Son,** established in 1900, is still run by the same family. This typically English and deliciously old-fashioned deli/restaurant is the perfect place to come for a tasty sandwich and a simple cup of tea.

35 marylebone lane, w1u, www.paulrotheandsondelicatessen.co.uk, t: 02079356783, open mon-fri 8am-6pm, sat 11am-5pm, price from £3.50, tube bond street

⑧ A trip to London is, of course, not complete without fish and chips, and you'd be hard-pressed to find any better than at **The Golden Hind.** This unassuming café has been around since 1914 and is still as popular as ever.

73 marylebone lane, w1u, t: 02074863644, open mon-fri noon-3pm & 6pm-10pm, sat 6pm-10pm, price £7, tube bond street

⑨ For a healthy pick-me-up, head to **Roots and Bulbs.** This juice bar serves fresh-pressed juices and smoothies, as well as super-healthy options like wheat grass and coconut water. Health-food fans can come here for their daily dose of power foods like quinoa salad, chia seeds, and almond milk.

5 thayer street, w1u, www.rootsandbulbs.com, t: 02074872900, open mon-fri 7:30am-6:30pm, sat-sun 10am-5pm, price £6, tube bond street

⑫ **The Providores & Tapa Room** is a long-running hit. Though always busy, the sensational Asian-Australian food at the Tapa Room is certainly worth the wait. Upstairs, The Providores restaurant serves more complex meals, making it the perfect place for a special occasion.

109 marylebone high street, w1u, www.theprovidores.co.uk, t: 02079356175, the providores open mon-fri noon-2:45pm & 6pm-10:30pm, sat 10am-2:45pm & 6pm-10:30pm, sun 10am-2:45pm & 6pm-10pm, tapa room open mon-fri 9am-10:30pm, sat 9am-3pm & 4pm-10:30pm, sun 9am-3pm & 4pm-10pm, price two-course meal £33, tube baker street/bond street

⑭ There are a limited number of tables at **La Fromagerie** cheese shop and deli, and they never stay open long. If you can get a table, choose from a variety of delicious dishes. The cheese platter is always an excellent option.

2-6 moxon street, w1u, www.lafromagerie.co.uk, t: 02079350341, open mon-fri 8am-7:30pm, sat 9am-7pm, sun 10am-6pm, price £8, tube baker street/bond street

⑯ **The Natural Kitchen** is a grocery store where everything is fresh, seasonal, organic, or handmade. You'll also find superfoods and gluten-free products here. You can come here any time of day for a bite to eat or something to drink. There are more tables in the back if there's no room in front. A café is upstairs.
77-78 marylebone high street, w1u, www.thenaturalkitchen.com, t: 02036966910, open mon-fri 7am-8pm, sat-sun 8am-7pm, price £6, tube baker street

㉕ In the bar at Gordon Ramsay's hotel **York & Albany** you can eat fresh brick-oven pizza and sip cocktails, beer, or a good glass of wine. If you'd prefer a more extensive dinner, you can order off the menu from the hotel restaurant.
127-129 parkway, nw1, www.gordonramsayrestaurants.com, t: 02075921227, open daily 7am-11am & noon-3pm & 6pm-midnight, price £19, tube camden town/mornington crescent

㉘ **Odette's** is a favorite spot among romantic locals. Both the restaurant and bar are particularly charming, and the modern British dishes go beyond your everyday fare. One taste and you'll understand why chef Bryn Williams was selected to prepare a birthday banquet for Queen Elizabeth. This is a great spot for a special dinner, but be sure to reserve a table in advance.
130 regent's park road, nw1, www.odettesprimrosehill.com, t: 02075868569, open tue-fri noon-2:30pm & 6pm-10pm, sat noon-3pm & 6pm-10:30pm, sun noon-3pm & 6pm-9:30pm, price £20, tube chalk farm

㉙ If you've got a penchant for desserts, take note: **Sweet Things** sells the best cakes, brownies, and cupcakes in London. This store/café has won various prizes, and the fudgy chocolate brownies are to die for.
138 regent's park road, nw1, www.sweetthings.biz, t: 02077222107, open mon-fri 8:30am-5pm, sat-sun 9:30am-6pm, tube chalk farm

㉚ **Lemonia** is a charming restaurant serving Greek fare. It is very popular among the locals. If you can't decide what to order, opt for the *mezze,* and they'll fill your table with a variety of tasty bites.
89 regent's park road, nw1, www.lemonia.co.uk, t: 02075867454, open mon-fri noon-3pm & 6pm-11:30pm, sat 6pm-11:30pm, sun noon-3pm, price set meal £25, tube chalk farm

③ Vegetarians are all too often stuck choosing between one or two menu options, but not at **Manna.** The menu here offers only delicious, creative vegetarian dishes. Try the falafel slider, enchilada lasagna, or organic bangers and mash. This is also a great choice for non-vegetarians who are willing to forgo meat for a meal.

4 erskine road, nw3, www.mannav.com, t: 02077228028, open tue-fri noon-3pm & 6:30pm-10pm, sat noon-3pm & 6pm-10pm, sun noon-8:30pm, price £14, tube chalk farm

③ **Greenberry Café** is a delightful neighborhood restaurant: Great for a cup of coffee or a good glass of wine, as well as a quick bite or a full meal. They serve dishes such as mushroom risotto and chicken breast with Greek yogurt and flatbread. At lunchtime, the restaurant is usually hopping with local residents, business owners, and moms. When it's really busy, they are not likely to seat you if you're only having a drink.

101 regent's park road, nw1, www.greenberrycafe.co.uk, t: 02074833765, open mon 9am-4:30pm, tue-sat 9am-10pm, sun 9am-4pm, price £15, tube chalk farm

③ **The Lansdowne** is a shabby-chic restaurant that is very popular among the local "yummy mummies" and their kids. Come here for quiche with chicory, onions, and goat cheese, or *steak frites*. Regardless of what you order, you're certain to enjoy the laidback atmosphere here. There are pizzas on the menu for kids.

90 gloucester avenue, nw1, www.thelansdownepub.co.uk, t: 02074830409, open mon-sat noon-11pm, sun noon-10:30pm, price £15, tube chalk farm

③ **Melrose & Morgan** is a deli where you'll be tempted to buy all types of jars and packages of scrumptious treats you never knew you needed. You can get a delicious breakfast or lunch in the café. The menu includes various soups, frittatas, and sandwiches made with artisanal sourdough bread. Whenever possible, seasonal and local ingredients are used.

42 gloucester avenue, nw1, www.melroseandmorgan.com, t: 02077220011, open mon-fri 8am-7pm, sat 8am-6pm, sun 9am-5pm, price £6, tube chalk farm

SHOPPING

(1) The largest and undoubtedly busiest shopping street in Europe is **Oxford Street.** All of the main retail outlets have stores here. You'll find names like TopShop, H&M, Gap, Zara, Urban Outfitters, Primark, River Island, Uniqlo, and Marks & Spencer all conveniently next to each other here.

oxford street, w1, www.oxfordstreet.co.uk, open mon-wed & fri 9:30am-8pm, thu 9am-10pm, sat 9am-9pm, sun noon-6pm, tube marble arch/bond street/oxford circus

(2) There are a variety of department stores on Oxford Street, but **Selfridges** is a favorite among Londoners. Come here for food, designer clothes, shoes, make-up, gadgets, home accessories, and much more. Among all of the beautiful objects for sale you'll also find a variety of restaurants and cafés.

400 oxford street, w1a, www.selfridges.com, t: 01133698040, open mon-sat 9:30am-10pm, sun 11:30am-6pm, tube bond street/marble arch

(5) **Tracey Neuls** uses old-fashioned techniques to turn simple women's shoes into ultra-modern works of art in a way that is timeless rather than trendy. The store interior is truly exceptional, with unique displays for all the shoes.

29 marylebone lane, w1u, www.traceyneuls.com, t: 02079350039, open mon-fri 11am-6:30pm, sat-sun noon-5pm, tube bond street

(7) **Content Beauty/Wellbeing** is filled top to bottom with natural, high-end personal care products you won't find anywhere else. Downstairs you can indulge in a beauty treatment.

14 bulstrode street, w1u, www.beingcontent.com, t: 02030751006, open mon-fri 10am-7pm, sat 10am-6pm, tube bond street

(10) The founder of *Wallpaper* is also responsible for **Monocle** and the eponymous magazine. In this tiny shop you'll find accessories, books, clothes, fragrances, and other beautiful objects, all of which have been specially designed for Monocle, by big names such as Bill Amberg, Havaianas, and Aspesi.

2a george street, w1u, www.monocle.com, t: 02074868770, open mon-sat 11am-7pm, sun noon-5pm, tube bond street

⑬ **The White Company** is highly recommended if you're looking for anything related to beds and baths. Farther up the road you'll find the Little White Company, selling great pajamas, bathrobes, slippers, and linens for little ones.

12 marylebone high street, w1u, www.thewhitecompany.com, t: 02079357879, open mon-sat 10am-6:30pm, sun noon-6pm, tube baker street/bond street

⑮ A trip to **Daunt Books** is worth it if for nothing else than to check out the beautiful historical building and take in the great atmosphere. The store has an excellent collection of travel books.

83 marylebone high street, w1u, www.dauntbooks.co.uk, t: 02072242295, open mon-sat 9am-7:30pm, sun 11am-6pm, tube baker street/bond street

⑰ For wonderful fragrances, go to **Le Labo.** The perfumes are mixed right here in the store. The fragrances are set but the ingredients are mixed together on the spot, which means you'll always have a fresh perfume. You can choose from natural scents such as jasmine, patchouli, fig, and musk. The oils, creams, and scented candles also smell divine.

28a devonshire street, w1g, www.lelabofragrances.com, t: 02034411535, open mon-wed & fri-sat 10am-6:30pm, thu 10am-7pm, sun noon-5pm, tube baker street

⑱ Colorful items with a hint of nostalgia fill the space at **Cath Kidston.** Here you'll find bags, dinnerware, table clothes, baby clothes, toys, and much more for the home, all decorated with the store's trademark colorful prints.

51 marylebone high street, w1u, www.cathkidston.co.uk, t: 02079356555, open mon-sat 10am-7pm, sun 11am-5pm, tube baker street/regent's park

⑲ For stylish furniture, kitchen accessories, and glasswork, **The Conran Shop** is an absolute must. You'll have to try hard if you want to leave the store empty-handed. Downstairs you'll find The Conran Kitchen, where you can get a nice cup of coffee and a sandwich or a yummy piece of cake.

55 marylebone high street, w1u, www.theconranshop.co.uk, t: 02077232223, open mon-sat 10am-7pm, sun 11am-6pm, tube baker street

㉑ To get to **Alfies Antique Market** you'll have to deviate from the designated walking route, but it's definitely worth the detour. This is a true treasure trove for anyone who loves antiques and vintage items. More than 100 vendors sell their wares in this enormous covered labyrinth, from teaspoons to sideboards. Tin Tin Collectables is a great spot for vintage clothing, and model Kate Moss is regularly spotted here. At the Rooftop Kitchen you can get a classic English breakfast or lunch.

13-25 church street, nw8, www.alfiesantiques.com, t: 02077236066, open tue-sat 10am-6pm, tube edgware road/marylebone

(33) **Tann Rokka** offers an extraordinary collection of extravagant antiques, modern accessories, furniture, and other luxury items for the home. It also has its own fragrance line. Featuring an in-store espresso and juice bar, this is always a great place to come and look around.

123 regent's park road, nw1, www.tannrokka.com, t: 02077223999, open mon-wed by appointment, thu-sun 10am-6pm, tube chalk farm

MORE TO EXPLORE

(3) Escape the shopping masses on Oxford Street and discover **St. Christopher's Place.** On this charming square and street you'll find a mix of one-of-a-kind stores, cafés, and restaurants. For wooden toys, head to Petit Chou, and visit Café Creperie for sweet and savory crêpes. In addition to the small, independent stores, around the corner you'll find a number of big British fashion retailers, including Reiss, Jigsaw, Whistles, and Phase Eight.

st. christopher's place, w1u, www.stchristophersplace.com, open daily, tube bond street

(23) You could easily spend the entire day at the gorgeous **Regent's Park.** Surrounded by beautiful stately buildings, the park offers something for everyone, from the Open Air Theatre and rose gardens to boat rides and the London Zoo.

regent's park, nw1, www.royalparks.org.uk/parks/the-regents-park, t: 03000612300, www.openairtheatre.org, theatre t: 08448264242, park open daily 5am-9:30pm, theatre open afternoon and evening for summer shows, entrance £5-£23, tube baker street/regent's park/camden town

(24) During the summer season, the **Open Air Theatre** offers a wonderful opportunity to enjoy productions of opera, ballet, and Shakespeare in the park. This landmark theater is a firm fixture of summer in the city, and the shows are considered one of London's cultural highlights.

regent's park, nw1, www.openairtheatre.org, t: 08448264242, open for afternoon and evening shows during the summer, entrance £5-£23, tube baker street/regent's park

(26) You'll easily need an entire day to see all of the animals at the **London Zoo.** There are more than 12,000 individual animals and over 700 species here, in areas including a Gorilla Kingdom and Penguin Beach. The zoo sometimes organizes late-night hours in the summer, which include live shows, food, and a silent disco. These evenings are very popular and booking in advance is required.

regent's park, nw1, www.zsl.org/zsl-london-zoo, t: 02077223333, open daily 10am-5pm, entrance £22, tube chalk farm

(27) **Primrose Hill** is located at the northern edge of Regent's Park and offers a surprisingly wonderful view of London. Up at the top is a sign that explains everything that can be seen in the distance. This spot has been featured in numerous movies and books, including *Bridget Jones: The Edge of Reason.*

primrose hill, www.royalparks.org.uk/parks/the-regents-park, open daily 5am-9:30pm, free entrance, tube chalk farm

WALK **6**

KNIGHTSBRIDGE & CHELSEA

ABOUT THE WALK

This walk is long and varied. It takes you past great stores, coffee shops, and restaurants, but the main focus of this route is art and culture. You'll walk by major museums and famous sights. The first half through Hyde Park in particular is perfect for biking.

THE NEIGHBORHOODS

Chelsea and Knightsbridge were once two small, verdant towns located at a fair distance from the polluted capital. Today, however, these two upscale neighborhoods are part of southwest London.

Chelsea was the birthplace of Swinging London back when Mick Jagger and friends used to hang out in the area's swanky cafés and boutiques. King's Road was a real-life catwalk where the latest fashion trends were conceived. Not much is left of the Swinging Sixties today, and Chelsea is now synonymous with wealth and excess. Celebrities, investment bankers, brokers, and billionaires from around the world live in beautiful, renovated Victorian buildings here.

Knightsbridge is home to London's most expensive homes and some of the streets have the highest density of millionaires in the world. This is clearly reflected in the selection or stores and restaurants in the area. **Sloane Street** is bursting with expensive shops from top fashion labels. The famous **Harrods** and **Harvey Nichols** department stores are also located here.

An increasing number of buildings in the area are being purchased as investments by wealthy foreigners, primarily from Russia, China, and the Middle East. The result is that many buildings remain empty because their owners live abroad. Some neighborhoods are so full of empty buildings that they are known as ghost towns.

There is no shortage of nature and culture in this area. **Hyde Park** is one of London's biggest parks and is a great place to go walking, running, or biking. The many museums also make this a popular neighborhood among tourists. Three of the best museums in the world can be found here: The **Natural History Museum, Victoria & Albert Museum,** and **Science Museum.**

SHORT ON TIME? HERE ARE THE HIGHLIGHTS
**+ HYDE PARK + SCIENCE MUSEUM + VICTORIA & ALBERT MUSEUM
+ DUKE OF YORK SQUARE + HARVEY NICHOLS**

TIPS

// Varied walk—great for first-time visitors
// The many museums make this walk a perfect way to take in art and culture
// Also well-suited for cycling

SIGHTS & ATTRACTIONS

③ At the **Serpentine Gallery** in Hyde Park, you'll find changing exhibitions of contemporary art that always have people talking. Every Saturday there are free seminars and readings related to the exhibitions being held. There is also a good collection of art books in the gift shop.

kensington gardens, w2, www.serpentinegallery.org, t: 02074026075, open tue-sun 10am-6pm, free entrance, tube south kensington/knightsbridge/lancaster gate

④ **Kensington Palace** is where Princess Diana and Prince Charles previously lived. Today, William and Kate's family call this palace home. There are various tours offered and exhibitions on display here.

kensington gardens, w8, www.hrp.org.uk/kensingtonpalace, t: 02031666000, open daily mar-oct 10am-6pm, nov-feb 10am-5pm, entrance £17.50, tube high street kensington/queensway

⑥ The **Design Museum** is located in the former Commonwealth Institute on Kensington High Street. The building housing the museum is at least three times as big as the museum's previous space. The new building has two large exhibition halls, permanent collections, and a restaurant with a view out over Holland Park. The collections on display here focus on renewed commercial industrial designs, from the Coca Cola can to Tupperware, and even classic cars. They include the work of Hella Jongerius, Alvar Aalto, and Dame Zaha Hadid, among others.

224-238 kensington high street, www.designmuseum.org, t: 02074036933, open daily 10am-6pm, free entrance to permanent collection, temporary exhibitions from £10, tube london bridge/tower hill

⑧ The **Science Museum** focuses on the history of science, from space travel to medicine. It also follows the evolution over time of the latest digital technologies. There are lots of fun, educational activities organized for kids.

exhibition road, south kensington, sw7, www.sciencemuseum.org.uk, t: 08708704868, open daily 10am-6pm, free entrance to permanent exhibitions, tube south kensington

⑨ You can see dinosaurs, volcanoes, fossils, stones, and a variety of animal species at the **Natural History Museum.** This museum is located in a beautiful building and there is plenty for children to see and discover here.

cromwell road, sw7, www.nhm.ac.uk, t: 02079425000, open daily 10am-5:50pm, free entrance to permanent exhibitions, tube south kensington

⑩ The **Victoria & Albert Museum** houses exhibits on fashion, architecture, photography, furniture, glass, ceramics, and much more. Items here cover a period of some 3,000 years. In addition to their permanent collection, the museum also has excellent temporary exhibitions. Be sure to stop by the gift shop and the courtyard for afternoon tea.

cromwell road, sw7, www.vam.ac.uk, t: 02079422000, open sat-thu 10am-5:45pm, fri 10am-10pm, free entrance to permanent collection, tube south kensington

㉘ Crazy about contemporary art? Then you must visit the enormous **Saatchi Gallery,** where you can see regularly changing exhibitions with works by emerging and established artists never or rarely exhibited in the UK.

duke of york's hq, king's road chelsea, sw3, www.saatchi-gallery.co.uk, t: 02078113085, open daily 10am-6pm, free entrance, tube sloane square

FOOD & DRINK

② **Serpentine Bar & Kitchen** is a fabulous café on the lake in Hyde Park. This is a great spot to start the day with a delicious breakfast. Or come here at the end of the day to see the sunset in a particularly romantic setting.

serpentine road, hyde park, w2, www.serpentinebarandkitchen.com, t: 02077068114, open daily 8am-9pm, price £10, tube knightsbridge

⑤ **The Orangery** serves delicious classic afternoon tea in an idyllic setting. The menu includes different types of teas, cakes, and sandwiches, as well as breakfast and lunch items. The castle gardens are also a wonderful place to sit.

kensington palace, kensington palace gardens, w8, www.orangerykensingtonpalace. co.uk, t: 02031666113, open daily 10am-6pm, price afternoon tea £26, tube high street kensington/queensway

⑫ London certainly has no shortage of great places to eat, and **Fernandez & Wells** is among locals' favorites. Order a strong espresso and a freshly made sandwich or settle down in the afternoon for a glass of wine and a well-deserved cheese platter. This is the ideal spot to come after a museum visit.

8 exhibition road, sw7, www.fernandezandwells.com, t: 02034901121, open mon-sat 8am-11pm, sun 8am-8pm, price £7.50, tube south kensington

⑬ **Comptoir Libanais** is the perfect place to relax after exploring a museum. This Lebanese restaurant offers generous plates of *mezze,* tajines, and tasty wraps with yummy dips. Everything is meant to be shared. Try the fresh lemonades, such as pomegranate and orange flower. This is also a great spot for breakfast.

1-5 exhibition road, sw7, www.lecomptoir.co.uk, t: 02072255006, open mon-sat 8:30am-midnight, sun 8:30am-10:30pm, price £8, tube south kensington

⑭ Tucked away down a small street behind King's Road you'll find **The Builders Arms.** This gastropub is an ideal spot for a drink and to mix with the Chelsea locals. You can also come here for lunch—the menu includes typical pub food.

13 britten street, sw3, www.geronimo-inns.co.uk/thebuildersarms, t: 02073499040, open mon-wed noon-11pm, thu-fri noon-midnight, sun noon-10:30pm, price £12, tube south kensington

⑮ For a great meal of delicious British fare, head to **Bumpkin.** The menu changes regularly because everything is made with seasonal ingredients, but expect classics such as shepherd's pie, fish and chips, and sticky toffee pudding.

119 sydney street, sw3, www.bumpkinuk.com, t: 02037309344, open mon-fri 11am-11pm, sat-sun 10am-midnight, price £15, tube south kensington/sloane square

⑲ If you're in the mood for a beer, there is no better place in this area than **The Pig's Ear.** Stay for dinner, too, if you're so inclined. The menu offers excellent dishes like risotto, steak, and grilled sardines.

35 old church street, sw3, www.thepigsear.info, t: 02073522908, open mon-fri noon-3pm & 6pm-10pm, sat noon-11pm, sun noon-9pm, price £15, tube sloane square

㉒ **Gordon Ramsay** is London's best-known chef. His eponymous restaurant is one of two in the city with three Michelin stars. Reserving a table here is no easy task. You have the greatest chance of getting a spot at lunchtime. Persistence pays off; an unforgettable culinary experience awaits you here. Aspiring chefs can also book a master class, and learn to create a specially selected three course lunch menu, chosen from a range of signature dishes.

68 royal hospital road, sw3, www.gordonramsay.com, t: 02073524441, open mon-fri noon-2:30pm & 6:30pm-11pm, price three-course lunch £45, three-course dinner £90, master class £600-£900, tube sloane square

㉚ Come to **The Botanist** any time of the day for lunch, afternoon tea, appetizers, dinner, or cocktails. This spot is as much about seeing and being seen as it is about the menu. Be sure to take a look at the restaurant's eye-catching hand-painted glass wall of natural history designs.

7 sloane square, sw1w, www.thebotanistonsloanesquare.com, t: 02077300077, open daily noon-11pm, price £20, tube sloane square

㉞ **Bar Boulud** is located in the Mandarin Oriental Hotel. Just as in its New York counterpart, this restaurant serves up classic French bistro fare. They also have delicious hamburgers and an extensive selection of charcuterie.

66 knightsbridge, sw1x, www.barboulud.com, t: 02072013899, open restaurant mon-sat noon-11pm, sun noon-10pm, price £23, tube knightsbridge

㉟ **The Berkeley** is a gorgeous hotel with a rooftop pool. The designer afternoon tea in the Caramel Room is a delightful surprise. Referred to as Prêt-à-Portea, the experience involves cakes and cookies in the shape of bags and shoes, and changes every six months. This is a fabulous treat for fashionistas.

wilton place, sw1x, www.the-berkeley.co.uk, t: 02072356000, prêt-à-portea open daily 1pm-5:30pm, price £45, tube knightsbridge/hyde park corner

SHOPPING

⑪ If you love interior design, then you absolutely must stop by **Mint.** This store has a thoughtful collection of home accessories and furniture from famous names and unknown designers alike, with prices ranging from affordable to super expensive. One thing's for sure: All items are completely original.

2 north terrace, alexander square, sw3, www.mintshop.co.uk, t: 02072252228, open mon-wed & fri-sat 10:30am-6:30pm, thu 10:30am-7:30pm, tube south kensington/knightsbridge

(17) **Orla Kiely**'s creations are known for their use of color and floral prints with a vintage twist. The Irish designer has lived and worked in London for years now and has two stores here. In addition to designing clothes, Orla also designs home and fashion accessories.

207 king's road, sw3, www.orlakiely.com, t: 02073512644, open mon-sat 10am-6:30pm, sun noon-5pm, tube south kensington/sloane square

(18) **Designers Guild,** known for its colorful fabrics, has a beautiful shop displaying the entire collection. Here you'll find furniture, towels, linens, dinnerware, pillows, wallpaper, and hundreds of fabrics.

267-277 king's road, sw3, www.designersguild.com, t: 02073515775, open mon-sat 10am-6pm, sun noon-5pm (fabric store closed sun), tube south kensington/sloane square

(20) **Shop at Bluebird** is part boutique, part gallery, part beauty salon. Here you'll find an inspiring collection of clothes, books, and furniture that revives the character of the Swinging '60s. The home accessories from Atelier Abigail Ahern are particularly beautiful. You can also get a manicure or pedicure here.

350 king's road, sw3, www.theshopatbluebird.com, t: 02073513873, open mon-sat 10am-7pm, sun noon-6pm, tube south kensington/sloane square

(23) Popular in the US, **Anthropologie** has crossed the pond and now has locations in the UK. The store on King's Road was one of the first European locations and was welcomed by Londoners with great enthusiasm. The beautiful building, which previously housed an antique dealer, offers a unique collection of women's clothes, accessories, and objects for the home. The store also has locations on Regent Street and in Marylebone High Street.

131-141 king's road, sw3, www.anthropologie.eu, t: 02073493110, open mon-sat 10am-7pm, sun noon-6pm, tube sloane square/south kensington

㉔ **Penhaligon**'s is the place to go for unique English perfumes in old-fashioned bottles. Here you'll find Winston Churchill's favorite fragrance and a number of historical scents dating back as far as 1927. They also offer a selection of bath oils, soaps, and other great accessories. This perfume store has retail outlets throughout the city and in some of the higher-end department stores.

132 king's road, sw3, www.penhaligons.com, t: 02078239733, open mon-tue & thu-sat 9:30am-6:30pm, wed 9:30am-7pm, sun noon-6:30pm, tube sloane square/south kensington

㉕ At **Neal's Yard Remedies,** health and beauty go hand in hand. In addition to an extensive collection of personal care products, the store also offers a number of natural remedies in the form of fragrant oils, herbs, and aromatherapy. Head to the beauty salon for a massage, facial, or acupuncture.

124b king's road sw3, www.nealsyardremedies.com, t: 02072252842, open mon-sat 10am-7pm, sun 10am-6pm, tube sloane square

㉖ **John Sandoe Books** is London's number-one independent literary bookstore. This is the perfect place to browse the stacks of books, and is especially good for when you need to find that one book you just can't get anywhere else.

10 blacklands terrace, sw3, www.johnsandoe.com, t: 02075899473, open mon-sat 9:30am-6:30pm, sun 11am-5pm, tube sloane square

㉜ **Sloane Street** is a super expensive shopping street, with high-end stores such as Chloé, Cartier, Gucci, Louis Vuitton, Chanel, and Valentino. If these brands are what you are looking for, you should also check out Old and New Bond Streets.

sloane street, sw1, www.sloane-street.co.uk, open mon-sat 10am-6pm, tube knightsbridge/sloane square

㉝ The fashion-conscious shop at **Harvey Nichols,** where you can find all of the best-known, exclusive fashion labels. The fifth floor is entirely dedicated to food and has a deli, restaurants, and a great terrace.

109-125 knightsbridge, sw1x, www.harveynichols.com, t: 02072355000, open mon-fri 10am-9pm, sun 11:30am-6pm, tube knightsbridge

㊱ London's best-known shopping attraction is hands-down the large **Harrods** department store. While perhaps best known for its specialty foods department, Harrods also has a great selection of high-end clothing, bags, cosmetics, toys, furniture, and more. You're likely to find more tourists here than Londoners. The store's large, extravagant Christmas department is typically British, and starting in August you can shop till you drop for tree ornaments and other holiday items.
87-135 brompton road, sw1x, www.harrods.com, t: 02077301234, open mon-sat 10am-9pm, sun 11:30am-6pm, tube knightsbridge

MORE TO EXPLORE

① **Hyde Park** is an enormous green space that is perfect for skating, biking, horseback riding, walking, or picnicking. You can also rent one of the many deck chairs here and just relax. In the middle of the park is Serpentine Lake, which is full of swans, ducks, and other water birds. You can also swim or rent a rowboat. Since 1872 the northeast side of Hyde Park, known as the Speakers' Corner, has been where people get on soapboxes and speak their minds. Anything goes, which can lead to some funny scenes. If you're with your kids, be sure to visit the Diana Princess of Wales Memorial Playground in the northwest corner of the park. This giant playground comes complete with a pirate ship and teepees.
hyde park, www.royalparks.org.uk/parks/hyde-park, t: 02072982100, open 5am-midnight, free entrance, tube hyde park corner/knightsbridge

⑦ You can see all types of concerts and ballet performances at the impressive **Royal Albert Hall.** The annual series of classical concerts, the Proms, is very popular, so be sure to book your tickets well in advance.
kensington gore, sw7, www.royalalberthall.com, t: 02075898212, opening hours and prices vary based on concerts/performances, tube south kensington

⑯ The **Chelsea Farmers Market** is not a market at all, but rather a collection of charming restaurants and shops. This is an especially great place when the weather is nice, and there is something here for everyone.
sydney street, sw3, www.chelseafarmersmkt.org, open daily, tube sloane square/ south kensington

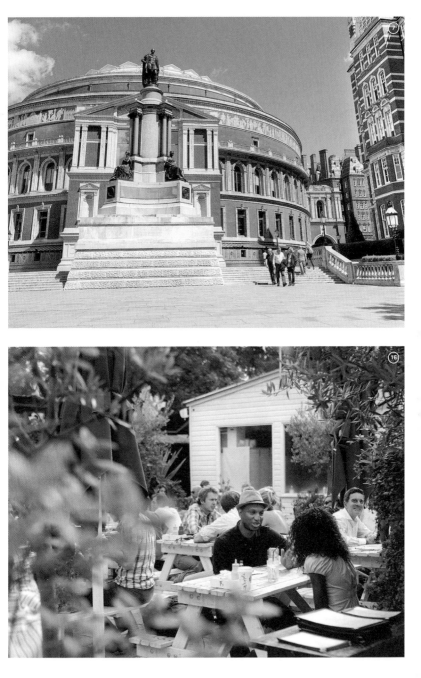

㉑ The **Chelsea Physic Garden** has been around since 1673, and medicinal and rare plants still flourish here. This secret spot is the perfect place to escape from the hustle and bustle of the big city. Get a drink or a small bite to eat in the Tangerine Dream Café. This is an especially nice spot for afternoon tea.

66 royal hospital road, sw3, www.chelseaphysicgarden.co.uk, t: 02073525646, open apr-oct tue-fri & sun 11am-6pm, nov-mar mon-fri 9:30am-4pm or sunset, café closed nov-mar, entrance £9.90, tube sloane square

㉗ The pedestrian-only square **Duke of York Square** is an unexpected oasis of calm with an extensive selection of outdoor eating establishments. The area also offers great shopping. Patisserie Valerie is recommended for a sweet fix, and Manicomio is great for a more elaborate lunch. The shops include everything from small boutiques to larger stores. Taschen is wonderful for beautiful books, Trilogy for trendy jeans, and Space NK Apothecary for beauty products.

duke of york square, sw3, www.dukeofyorksquare.com, open daily, tube sloane square

㉙ **Royal Court Theatre** is known for its top-quality performances that always get people talking. New writers and plays are given a great platform here. Theater aficionados should check the website to see what is playing.

sloane square, sw1w, www.royalcourttheatre.com, t: 02075655000, open daily, price tickets from £12, £10 on mon, tube sloane square

㉛ More than 300 concerts and events are held annually at **Cadogan Hall.** These performances are mostly classical music concerts, plus the BBC Proms. The space is also the home base of the Royal Philharmonic Orchestra.

5 sloane terrace, sw1x, www.cadoganhall.com, t: 02077304500, hours vary based on performances, tube sloane square

WITH MORE TIME

The walks in this book will take you to most of the city's main highlights. Yet there are still a number of sights worth seeing that are not included in these walks. These are listed here. While not all of these places are easily accessible by foot from in town, you can get to all of them using public transportation.

Ⓐ If you're interested in all things green, **Kew Gardens** is not to be missed. The botanic gardens have been around for over 200 years and are located a short ways outside of the city. Plan a full day for your visit to the largest collection of living plants in the world. On rainy days, head to the Palm House—an indoor rainforest. If time permits, check out the surrounding town of Richmond.

kew, richmond, www.kew.org, t: 02083325655, open mon-fri 10am-6:30pm, sat-sun 10am-7:30pm, entrance £15, tube or train kew gardens

Ⓑ **Covent Garden** is known as the entertainment center of London. The area is characterized by its many tourists and street performers. People must audition to perform here, so you can expect a good show. You'll also find dozens of places to eat or drink, lots of theaters, and the wonderful London Transport Museum, plus myriad shopping opportunities. Start at the Covent Garden Piazza and use that as your orientation point. You'll find clothes on Floral Street, shops catering to younger crowds on Neal Street, and vegetarian food options at Neal's Yard.

covent garden, wc2, www.coventgardenlondonuk.com, t: 02078369136, tube covent garden

Ⓒ **Notting Hill** has been more popular than ever since the release of the name-sake movie. Don't come here for culture, but rather to enjoy the great atmosphere. The neighborhood is full of charming shops and restaurants, such as those on Westbourne Grove. Also check out the **Portobello Road Market.** You won't find any bargains here, but it's a unique experience. There are different goods on offer every day. Antiques are available on Saturdays, when the market is expanded. The farther down the street you go, the more unique the offerings become, so don't be put off by the somewhat-shabby overpass.

portobello road, w11, www.thehill.co.uk, market open mon-wed & sat 8am-6:30pm, thu 8am-1pm, tube notting hill gate/ladbroke grove

Ⓓ Londoners come to **Greenwich** to escape the hustle and bustle of downtown London. It's right on the Thames and feels almost like a seaside town. Come here by boat to really get in the mood for your visit. Once back on land you can stroll through the markets and stop for a bite in any of the charming restaurants. Greenwich's historic center has been declared a World Heritage Site, and culture abounds. There are numerous beautiful old buildings in the picturesque Greenwich Park, such as the Royal Observatory, where you'll find the Prime Meridian. The Maritime Museum, *Cutty Sark,* and the Old Royal Naval College are also worth visiting. The Emirates Air Line is good fun too, and in five minutes the cable car can shuttle you between the O2 Arena on the Greenwich Peninsula and the Royal Docks. The view as it takes you over the Thames is amazing.
www.visitgreenwich.org.uk, dlr greenwich

Ⓔ From Greenwich, it's pleasant to take a trip over to **Canary Wharf.** You board a boat in what feels like a small town and step out in the big city, among the skyscrapers of the Docklands. Here in London's new financial center, you'll find modern apartment buildings, renovated warehouses, the docks, great outdoor eating establishments, and a plethora of shopping opportunities—not to mention very few tourists. During the week, Canary Wharf is primarily full of sharply dressed professionals rushing from one meeting to another and stopping to enjoy a nice lunch in the sun when time allows.

www.canarywharf.com, tube canary wharf

(F) If you're in the mood for some fresh air, head to **Hampstead Heath.** This nature reserve in the north of London contains numerous ponds, hills, parks, and woods. Londoners like to come here to walk and run, and to enjoy the breathtaking views of the city. Nearby Hampstead Village is a charming neighborhood with a small-town feel and lots of great places for shopping, eating, and getting a drink.

www.hampsteadheath.net, tube hampstead

(G) **Somerset House** is a center for arts and culture. In this historic building you'll find exhibitions on art and design. The Courtauld Gallery in particular has an impressive collection of world-famous paintings from artists such as Renoir, Monet, and Gauguin. During the summer, open-air concerts, movies, and tours are organized in the courtyard, and the space is transformed into an ice-skating rink in the winter. Somerset House is also home to London Fashion Week, when fashion lovers from around the globe come together to take in the latest shows. For two weeks a year, this is the number-one place in London to see and be seen.

strand, wc2r, www.somersethouse.org.uk, t: 02078454600, open daily 8am-6pm, price courtauld gallery £7, tube temple, covent garden

(H) For a spectacular view of London, a visit to **The Shard** is highly recommended. Although opinions are split on the aesthetic qualities of Western Europe's tallest building, everyone agrees that the view from the top is absolutely stunning. A high-speed elevator brings you up to the top of the building, and from the 69th floor and a height of 800 feet you can look out over all of London. The Shard is home to the exclusive Shangri-La Hotel and a variety of great restaurants.

32 london bridge street, se1, www.theviewfromtheshard.com, t: 03444997222, open sun-wed 10am-7pm, thu-sat 10am-10pm, entrance £25.95, tube london bridge

Ⓘ At Warner Bros. Studios, Harry Potter fans can get a behind-the-scenes look at the making of the movies with the **Harry Potter Studio Tour.** See the costumes, props, and sets used in filming, including Hagrid's Hut and Diagon Alley, and learn about the various special effects. The tour lets you discover the magic behind the movies. The studios are in Watford, about 20 miles outside of central London, but the train ride out there is well worth it.

studio tour drive, leavesden, wd25 7lr, www.wbstudiotour.co.uk, t: 02073238299, open daily from 10am, last tour 6.30pm, price tickets £33, train watford junction

Ⓙ Following the 2012 Summer Games in London, the Olympic Park in Stratford was transformed into the **Queen Elizabeth Olympic Park.** This is one of London's largest green spaces and there's always something going on. Visit the stadium and other sports facilities where the Games were held. The park also has a variety of cafés and is home to the ArcelorMittal Orbit, an observation tower offering great views of the park and city.

stratford, e20 2st, www.queenelizabetholympicpark.co.uk, open daily, tube stratford

Ⓚ **Hayward Gallery** is a great place to check out innovative modern art. The exhibitions here are unique and thought-provoking and showcase the work of both well-known and lesser-known artists. The gallery opened in 1968 and is located close to the Thames.

southbank, se1, www.southbankcentre.co.uk/venues/hayward-gallery, t: 02079604200, open mon noon-6pm, tue-wed & sat-sun 11am-7pm, thu-fri 11am-8pm, entrance £15, tube waterloo

Ⓛ If you're lucky enough to get your hands on tickets for a show at the **National Theatre,** you're in for a great night out. Both large- and small-scale productions are presented here, and all are equally impressive. The theater is located in a large concrete building in the South Bank Centre on the Thames, and has three auditoriums, various restaurants and bars, and exhibition spaces. For a peek behind the scenes, book a backstage tour.

southbank, se1, www.nationaltheatre.org.uk, t: 02074523000, open mon-sat 9:30am-11pm, sun noon-6pm, price varies by production, tube waterloo

AFTER DARK

When it comes to nightlife, London is hands-down the top city in Europe. Music, movies, theater, comedy, opera, cabaret, dance—you name it, London's got it.

Soho is London's best-known area for nightlife. The neighborhood has numerous restaurants and charming pubs, along with plenty of theaters, cocktail bars, and nightclubs. Anything is possible here. Feel like a night at the theater? Head to Soho Theatre or the National Theatre. Tickets can be hard to get, however, so always try to book them in advance.

Other parts of the city that are good for a night of dancing or a nice drink are Shoreditch and Dalston. You'll find plenty of clubs and cocktail lounges to choose from.

You'll find the latest information about London's top spots for a night on the town on our website, from upscale cocktail and wine bars to local pubs and popular clubs. Check out **www.timetomomo.com** and plan your own perfect night out in London.

HOTELS

A comfortable bed, a tasty breakfast, and a nice interior are all essential ingredients for a pleasant hotel stay. Even more important, however, is location. A hotel is really only good if you can walk straight out of the lobby and into the bustling city.

Spending the night in central London can be pricey, but there are number of good options, such as The Tommyfield Hotel in Kennington. For those with a bigger budget, there's also the Great Northern Hotel and the Soho Hotel. Want to be able to roll out of a club and right into bed? Then consider a room at the Hoxton or the Ace Hotel in Shoreditch. If you'd rather wake up somewhere calmer, you'd probably prefer to stay in a neighborhood like Greenwich or Richmond.

INDEX

TRANSPORTATION

MOON LONDON WALKS

FIRST EDITION

Avalon Travel
An imprint of Perseus Books
A Hachette Book Group company
1700 Fourth Street
Berkeley, CA 94710, USA
www.moon.com

ISBN 978-1-63121-598-8

Concept & Original Publication "time to momo London" © 2017 by mo'media.
All rights reserved.
For the latest on time to momo walks and recommendations, visit www.timetomomo.com.

MO'MEDIA

TEXT & WALKS
Kim Snijders

TRANSLATION
Eileen Holland

MAPS
Van Oort redactie & kartografie

PHOTOGRAPHY
Marjolein den Hartog

DESIGN
Studio 100% & Oranje Vormgevers

PROJECT EDITORS
Heleen Ferdinandusse, Bambi Bogert

AVALON TRAVEL

PROJECT EDITOR
Sierra Machado

COPY EDITOR
Maggie Ryan

PROOFREADER
Janet Walden

EDITORIAL INTERN
Rachael Sablik

COVER DESIGN
Derek Thornton, Faceout Studios

Printed in China by RR Donnelley
First U.S. printing, September 2017.

100% good time

time to momo
LONDON

And to find out more about
the latest hot spots, best
hotels, nicest neighborhoods,
and where to have the most
fun in London, go to
www.timetomomo.com/london

Individual walks

app